the PRIORITY of PRAISE & WORSHIP

Learning to Give Back to God

DR. RON KENOLY

Parsons Publishing House
Your Voice Your World™

THE PRIORITY OF PRAISE AND WORSHIP
by Ron Kenoly

Parsons Publishing House
P. O. Box 6428
Panama City, FL 32404 USA
www.ParsonsPublishingHouse.com
Info@ParsonsPublishingHouse.com

All Scripture quotations, unless otherwise indicated, are taken from the Holy Bible, King James Version, Cambridge, 1769.

Cover Design by Diane Parsons

Printed in the United States of America.
For World-Wide Distribution.
Published by Parsons Publishing House.

International Standard Book Number:
13 digit: 978-1-60273-002-1
10 digit: 1-60273-002-4
Library of Congress Control Number: 2007928407

DEDICATION

To my mother, the late Edith Odessa Kenoly, a great woman of God, who believed from the time I was conceived that God had a special plan and purpose for my life. She encouraged me in every way and made many sacrifices to help me become the man of God I am today.

TABLE OF CONTENTS

INTRODUCTION

The Lord is worthy to receive all honor and respect as we praise and worship Him. Every Christian should prioritize praise and worship as one of the most important activities to perform in our spiritual lives. It will be through these actions where the Creator of the Universe is able to have an intimate and personal relationship with you. Through praise and worship, God will be able to transform you into His image. Let us journey together to learn of this priority, see the purpose and understand the power behind these holy and ordained directives.

CHAPTER 1

RELATIONSHIP
THE FIRST PRIORITY

T his book is about the priority of praise and worship in spirit and truth. Jesus reveals to us in the Gospel of John 4:24, in His dialogue with a Samaritan woman at a community well, *"God is a Spirit: and they that worship him must worship him in spirit and in truth."* In this conversation with a lowly and rejected woman, He brought us to a new understanding of how we are to worship God, our creator and Father. Not just in a certain place or with certain animal sacrifices, but with a heart full of love and devotion.

Jesus was initiating a new era of human relationship with God. He was restoring the concept of man to once again have a personal and intimate relationship with God through worship.

Since the fall of Adam and Eve, the only atonement for sin was to shed the blood of an animal and place the carcass on an altar to be consumed by fire. This act of bloodshed represented humility, sorrow and tribute to the One who created all things and is greater than all things that were created.

From the beginning of Genesis to the end of Revelation, the Bible has one central theme: God desiring to restore His relationship with humankind that He had with Adam and Eve in the Garden. From Genesis three to the end of the book of Revelation, the Bible message is all about God renewing the relationship He had with His special creation, man.

The Garden of Eden

God had created man and woman and placed them in the Garden of Eden. Genesis 2:8 records, *"And the Lord God planted a garden eastward in Eden; and there he put the man whom he had formed."* It was in this garden that they had fellowship with their creator; God communed with them on a continual basis. It was in this garden where they fellowshipped in the cool of the day.

The Lord gave specific instructions to Adam in the garden. We read in Genesis 2:15-17,

And the Lord God took the man, and put him into the Garden of Eden to dress it

and to keep it. And the Lord God com-
manded the man, saying, Of every tree
of the garden thou mayest freely eat: but
of the tree of the knowledge of good and
evil, thou shalt not eat of it: for in the
day that thou eatest thereof thou shalt
surely die.

Adam and Eve ate from the forbidden tree.
We read of this account in Genesis 3:6-7.

And when the woman saw that the tree
was good for food, and that it was pleas-
ant to the eyes, and a tree to be desired
to make one wise, she took of the fruit
thereof, and did eat, and gave also unto
her husband with her; and he did eat.
And the eyes of them both were opened,
and they knew that they were naked;
and they sewed fig leaves together, and
made themselves aprons.

Through disobedience, they sinned and the
result was separation from God. Both were cast
from this garden of paradise and away from the
presence of the Father. God had told them that
the day they ate from the tree of the knowledge of
good and evil they would die. From that point on,
man contaminated the holy relationship between
God and himself.

God's Presence Requires
a Holy Environment

One of the unique things we see about the creation is that God always created a perfect environment for everything He created. When He created the fish, He also created the water. Water, of course, is the optimum environment for the fish. Without water, a fish will soon die.

The same is true for the birds and flying animals. God created the air and atmospheric pressure so the birds could spread their wings and fly. Without the air, the birds could never be what the Creator intended for them to be. They could never do what He intended for them to do.

Consider the land animals. Without the fields and forests, the beasts could not sustain their life. Each one has its own particular habitat designed especially for its optimum existence.

The same is true for man. When God created Adam, He also created the Garden of Eden. God placed man in the garden because it was the most suitable place for the man to exist. This garden was special because it was holy; it was the place where God manifested His presence. God requires holiness before He manifests His presence. The optimum place for man is in God's presence. In the presence of God, man has the ability to live forever.

God never planned for man to die. His plan has always been for man to share eternity with Him. The Lord designed man to live forever. In the presence of the Father, there is life forever more.

God has been trying constantly to find a way to get the relationship back. We see throughout the Scriptures that worship is God's highest priority and that worship is the avenue to the heart of God. The Lord's desire is seen in Exodus 20:3-6:

> *Thou shalt have no other gods before me. Thou shalt not make unto thee any graven image, or any likeness of any thing that is in heaven above, or that is in the earth beneath, or that is in the water under the earth: thou shalt not bow down thyself to them, nor serve them: for I the Lord thy God am a jealous God, visiting the iniquity of the fathers upon the children unto the third and fourth generation of them that hate me; and shewing mercy unto thousands of them that love me, and keep my commandments.*

Praise and worship is the willful act that allows us to realize fellowship, audience, communion and companionship with God.

It is recorded in Exodus 3:12, *"And He said, Certainly I will be with thee; and this shall be a token unto thee, that I have sent thee: When thou hast brought forth the people out of Egypt, ye shall serve God upon this mountain.*" God heard the cries of His people in Egypt. They had been in Egypt for over four hundred years serving as slaves under harsh bondage. When it was time for His people to be delivered, Moses was chosen to be their deliverer. God's promise to Abraham, their ancestor, was that they would someday have a land of their own. He promised them a land that was fruitful with cities that they did not build. Exodus 2:23-25 says:

> *And it came to pass in process of time, that the king of Egypt died: and the children of Israel sighed by reason of the bondage, and they cried, and their cry came up unto God by reason of the bondage. And God heard their groaning, and God remembered his covenant with Abraham, with Isaac, and with Jacob. And God looked upon the children of Israel, and God had respect unto them.*

God would certainly bring deliverance to His people. He would also demonstrate to them that He would be their provider, healer, protector and champion in battle. The Lord declared the Israelite's freedom in Exodus 3:7-8.

> *And the Lord said, I have surely seen the affliction of my people which are in*

Egypt, and have heard their cry by reason of their taskmasters; for I know their sorrows; and I am come down to deliver them out of the hand of the Egyptians, and to bring them up out of that land unto a good land and a large, unto a land flowing with milk and honey; unto the place of the Canaanites, and the Hittites, and the Amorites, and the Perizzites, and the Hivites, and the Jebusites.

However, before he took them into the land of promise He told Moses to bring them to Mount Sinai to offer sacrifices and worship Him on that mountain.

The only examples of worship the children of Israel had were the examples they had seen in Egypt. Their previous captors, the Egyptians, worshiped animals, celestial bodies, ancestors, idols they had created and creatures that lived in or around the Nile River. The rituals of worship that the Egyptians performed were unacceptable to the God of creation.

Through Moses and Aaron, God had to teach His people the proper and appropriate way to worship and praise Him. It was on Mount Sinai that God gave instructions to Moses on how to create an environment for His holy presence. It was in and around the Tabernacle of Moses that

God revealed His presence by fire at night and a cloud by day.

To serve God, is to worship Him. If you are not a worshiper, you cannot enter into the presence of God. If you are not a worshiper, you cannot create an environment for the presence of God and you will never know Him. His desire is that we know Him. We were created to praise and worship Him and to fellowship with Him. Isaiah 43:21 reads, *"This people have I formed for myself; they shall shew forth my praise."*

God is holy. The word *holy* in the Old Testament means to cut away; to separate from uncleanness, corruption or contamination or to consecrate to what is pure. In Exodus 3:5 God expects us to acknowledge His holiness, *"And he said, Draw not nigh hither: put off thy shoes from off thy feet, for the place whereon thou standest is holy ground."*

Because of Adam's sin, all of mankind was born into sin and iniquity. Without the blood of Jesus, our lives are contaminated with sin. When we have sin in God's presence, the Lord would be contaminated. However, God cannot allow Himself to be contaminated or corrupt. The Lord provided a way for His people to be holy, set apart, clean and separated from all that is sinful and corrupt. We must rely on the sinless blood of Jesus to cleanse us from all unrighteousness.

God desires purity in each one of us. It is in our worship experience where we realize that purity allows us to come in contact with God. This knowledge of His holiness is why God desires each one of us to worship Him. The saving grace offered by Jesus allows us entrance into the Lord's presence; yet, worship is the key to that personal relationship with God the Father.

CHAPTER 2

WHAT DOES GOD RECEIVE FROM OUR CHURCH SERVICES?

What does God receive from a church gathering? Suppose we have a birthday party and you are the guest of honor. We're going to make sure that everyone is happy. There will be party favors, food and drinks and music to be enjoyed by all. We might have a dee-jay. Everyone is going to come to your party. We're going to enjoy the food. We're going to enjoy the music. We are going to enjoy the fellowship.

What would happen if we did not give you anything? How would you feel if we forgot to honor you with a cake? What would it be like if we did not sing "Happy Birthday" to you? Suppose you were ignored at this party that was planned in your name to give honor to you?

That is what happens when we come into a church service and we don't worship God appropriately. All of our church gatherings are supposed to honor God and celebrate His love and goodness to us. The party is in His honor and the appropriate response is for everyone to bring a gift and celebrate Him.

When we come together in our regular church services, everyone receives something. We're inspired by the sermon and blessed by a prayer. We're going to get encouraged by one another and the Word of God. We're going to fellowship and have a good time. We're going to eat the bread of life. Everyone is going to get something.

What is God going to get at this assembly? The preaching may be good. Praise God for the preaching, but that's for us. Preachers, you can't preach anything that God didn't give you. At least, I hope you don't. You can't tell God anything that He doesn't already know. You can prophesy, but you cannot prophesy anything that He didn't give you otherwise you are a lying and false prophet.

If you say, "I'm giving my money." Do not fool yourself. God has given you everything that you have. God has said that whatever you give, He is going to give back to you anyway. Luke 6:38 reads, *"Give, and it shall be given unto you; good measure, pressed down, and shaken together, and running over, shall men give into your bosom."*

You might say, "I'm a prayer intercessor." The prayers we pray are for our heavenly God to intervene in our earthly situations. Jesus is the great intercessor. 1 Timothy 2:5-6 says,

> *For there is one God, and one mediator between God and men, the man Christ Jesus; who gave himself a ransom for all, to be testified in due time.*

- The preaching is for us.
- The prophecy is for us.
- The healing is for us.
- The giving is for us.
- The fellowship is for us.
- The prayers are for us.

The Only Thing He Wants

The only thing that the Lord wants is the praise and the worship. Worship is the only appropriate gift that He desires. When we don't worship Him in spirit and in truth, we have insulted God. It is an insult for me to come to your party and not bring you a gift. How dare I show up at your party and not bring a gift to you. You would be insulted and sincerely disappointed.

Worship is the only appropriate gift that we can give to God. You can say, "God, I'm a singer." You can't impress God with your singing. Every gift comes from God so He is not impressed with all your vocal aerobics or the hot licks on your instrument. James 1:17 says, *"Every good gift and every perfect gift is from above, and cometh down from the Father of lights, with whom is no variableness, neither shadow of turning."*

God wants praise and worship in spirit and truth. The Bible says in John 4:23-24,

> *But the hour cometh, and now is, when the true worshipers shall worship the Father in spirit and in truth:* **for the Father seeketh such to worship him.** *God is a Spirit: and they that worship him must worship him in spirit and in truth.*

CHAPTER 3

WHY IS IT IMPORTANT TO WORSHIP GOD?

First of all: praise and worship is what God desires. His desire is for all of us to be true worshipers. When God finds a worshiper, He can make that person anything He needs them to be. Jesus said in John 4:23, *"God is a spirit and those that worship Him must worship Him in spirit and in truth."*

One of the key words in that passage of Scripture is *seeketh*. Have you ever lost your car keys or misplaced your wallet or purse? When you lose it, you look everywhere for that thing which is so important to you. You will move the couch and look under the pillows. You will look all over the floor and under the furniture. You look in the car, the bathroom and the kitchen. You will go to the closets and check the pockets of your clothes. You will look in your children's rooms. You will look everywhere. You may ask repeatedly, "Where did I leave those keys?" They are important to you.

With the same urgency, God is seeking or looking for worshipers. Worshipers are important to Him. **Worshipers are the people that the Lord uses to change the world.** True worshipers are the only ones God can trust to carry out His mandate in the earth. A true worshiper will always have God's interest in their hearts. Are you a worshiper? Are you the one that God is looking for?

God Needed a King

God needed to replace the king of Israel because King Saul was disobedient. God said, "This is not the man to lead my people. I need a king for my people." What did the Lord do? God scanned all over Judea and He found a teenager in the hills of Judea with a little instrument that he made himself to praise and worship God.

This boy was out in the pasture and watched over a flock of smelly, dirty sheep that belonged to his father. While this young man was caring for the sheep, he was writing songs of praise and worship to God. David wrote such songs as Psalms 8:1-9.

O Lord our Lord, how excellent is thy name in all the earth! who hast set thy glory above the heavens. Out of the mouth of babes and sucklings hast thou ordained strength because of thine enemies, that thou mightest still the enemy and the avenger. When I consider thy heavens, the work of thy fingers, the moon and the stars, which thou hast ordained; What is man, that thou art mindful of him? and the son of man, that thou visitest him? For thou hast made him a little lower than the angels, and hast crowned him with glory and honour. Thou madest him to have dominion over the works of thy hands; thou hast put all things under his feet: All sheep and oxen, yea, and the beasts of the field; The fowl of the air, and the fish of the sea, and whatsoever passeth through the paths of the seas. O Lord our Lord, how excellent is thy name in all the earth!

In Psalms 23:1-6, David, the shepherd boy, took courage in his God being the Great Shepherd.

The Lord is my shepherd; I shall not want. He maketh me to lie down in green pastures: he leadeth me beside the still waters. He restoreth my soul:

17

*he leadeth me in the paths of righteous-
ness for his name's sake. Yea, though I
walk through the valley of the shadow of
death, I will fear no evil: for thou art
with me; thy rod and thy staff they comfort me. Thou preparest a table before
me in the presence of mine enemies: thou
anointest my head with oil; my cup run-
neth over. Surely goodness and mercy
shall follow me all the days of my life:
and I will dwell in the house of the Lord
for ever.*

God said, "That's My King; he's a worshiper." We read in 1 Samuel 13:14 where it says,
*"The Lord hath sought him a man after his own
heart, and the Lord hath commanded him to be
captain over his people."*

Soon afterwards, the prophet Samuel went
to the house of David's father in Bethlehem. After
passing over all of Jesse's sons at home, Samuel
anointed David as king of Israel. David was a man
that God could use. Here was the man that God
desired to lead His people. Why? He was not the
tallest. He was not the strongest. He was not the
smartest. If the leader is a worshiper, he will
teach the people to be worshipers. David was a
man after God's heart. God could trust him to
obey and carry out His divine mandates and instructions. David was pliable and usable in the
Master's hands.

There is something very interesting about this story. Immediately after the anointing ceremony, the Spirit of the Lord came upon David. The Lord was with him. At this point, David was set apart and destined for greatness. He had the unquestionable favor of the Lord. It was not because of his size, talent or intelligence, but because of his love, respect and because he set his heart on pleasing and honoring God.

David did not immediately go to the palace and replace King Saul. No, he did just the opposite. David went right back to the hills and to his father's sheep for which he had previously cared. David was recognized by God as king of Israel, but he was still the same little shepherd boy to his family and friends. He left the sheep in the hills and answered the prophets call to be anointed king and went right back to the hills to keep watch over the sheep.

It was several years later when David was actually anointed king by the people of Judah. It would be several more years after the Lord anointed him as King of Judah that he would be anointed by the people as King over all of Israel and Judah.

Often it will take years for the plans of God to materialize. God never seems to be in a hurry and He is never late. The Lord allowed David to develop in stature and wisdom before He promoted him to the responsibility of being the shepherd of His chosen nation Israel. David never became prideful or puffed up about what God was doing in his life. He remained humbled and submitted to the plan and the will of God. David remained faithful to King Saul even though he knew that some day he would become the king of the nation.

An evil spirit came upon King Saul which caused him to try to kill David. Even through this, David remained faithful to the Lord's reigning king.

David not only had favor with God, but he also had favor with the people of the nation. The women sang songs about David's great exploits as a warrior and military leader. Many of the people wanted David to be their king. He was extremely popular and it was obvious that God was with him in all that he did.

A Lesson From the Life of David

We can all learn a lesson from the life of David. Many times, we are prophesied over or given a word of knowledge; we may think that God wants to elevate us at that very moment the prophecy is given. There are times when God will give us a dream or vision that pertains to our lives and callings. We often get excited and anxious about that glorious thing the Lord has revealed to us and we want these fantastic things to happen right now. However, the Father has His own timetable for blessing. Promotion comes from above and God will give promotions when only He will receive the glory.

A true worshiper will always submit to the plans and the timing of the Lord. A true worshiper will not try to steal or share any of the glory that belongs to God alone. Waiting on the Father is one of the elements of a true worship experience. When God promotes, it is always in His perfect timing and under the right circumstances. God sees the big picture. He knows the before and after. He knows when we are ready to face and overcome the events that are in our future.

God Needed a Warrior

God needed a warrior when Goliath, the Philistine giant, stood in the Valley of Elah and held all of the armies of Israel in terror. God needed someone to remove that man. Goliath was the terrorist of that time; he was the champion of the Philistines. He alone caused the armies of Israel to tremble in fear. 1 Samuel 17:10-11 tells of the confrontation.

> And the Philistine said, 'I defy the armies of Israel this day; give me a man, that we may fight together.' When Saul and all Israel heard those words of the Philistine, they were dismayed, and greatly afraid.

By divine appointment, David, the young shepherd boy, the worshiper, the anointed of God, showed up on the scene. When he heard the insults that were shouted at the Israeli army by this Philistine giant, David became upset and disturbed. We read in 1 Samuel 17:28-30:

> And Eliab his eldest brother heard when he spake unto the men; and Eliab's anger was kindled against David, and he said, Why camest thou down hither? and with whom hast thou left those few sheep in the wilderness? I know thy pride, and the naughtiness of thine heart; for thou art come down that thou mightest see the battle. And David said, What have I now done? Is there not a cause? And he turned from him toward another, and spake after the same manner: and the people answered him again after the former manner.

After getting permission from King Saul, David walked down into that valley with only a slingshot and five stones. The story continues in 1 Samuel 17:40-47.

> And he took his staff in his hand, and chose him five smooth stones out of the brook, and put them in a shepherd's bag which he had, even in a scrip; and his sling was in his hand: and he drew near

to the Philistine. And the Philistine came on and drew near unto David; and the man that bare the shield went before him. And when the Philistine looked about, and saw David, he disdained him: for he was but a youth, and ruddy, and of a fair countenance. And the Philistine said unto David, Am I a dog, that thou comest to me with staves? And the Philistine cursed David by his gods. And the Philistine said to David, Come to me, and I will give thy flesh unto the fowls of the air, and to the beasts of the field. Then said David to the Philistine, Thou comest to me with a sword, and with a spear, and with a shield: but I come to thee in the name of the Lord of hosts, the God of the armies of Israel, whom thou hast defied. This day will the Lord deliver thee into mine hand; and I will smite thee, and take thine head from thee; and I will give the carcasses of the host of the Philistines this day unto the fowls of the air, and to the wild beasts of the earth; that all the earth may know that there is a God in Israel. And all this assembly shall know that the Lord saveth not with sword and spear: for the battle is the Lord's, and he will give you into our hands.

When the Lord needed a warrior, He chose His worshiper. God knew that He could trust His worshiper. David had full faith and confidence that by the power of God, he would kill the giant and demonstrate that the God of Israel is the true and almighty God. The Lord knew that David was not hungry for glory himself. God knew that David would bring honor and praise to Jehovah for any and all victories.

True worshipers are not concerned about glory for themselves. They know and understand that God, and God alone, is the One who gives us the ability to accomplish great and mighty things. God specializes in things that the world considers impossible. He will choose the least of us to do things that amaze the world because He will receive the glory.

When God Needed a Priest

During the time of Eli the high priest, the Ark of the Covenant had been taken by the Philistine army into the battle. In 1 Samuel 4:10-11, we see:

> And the Philistines fought, and Israel was smitten, and they fled every man into his tent: and there was a very great slaughter; for there fell of Israel thirty thousand footmen. And the ark of God was taken; and the two sons of Eli, Hophni and Phinehas, were slain.

The Ark of the Covenant represented the presence of God. When the Philistines captured the Ark of the Covenant, they placed it near their god Dagon in the house of Dagon. When the Philistines went into the house of Dagon, they found that the statue of Dagon had fallen on his face before the Ark of God. Even the idol god of the Philistines could not stand in the presence of the Most High God of the Israelites.

Fear came upon the Philistines because the Lord God Jehovah caused tumors to come upon the people of Philistia. They were afraid that the same plagues which came upon the Egyptians would come on them. All of the nations of that region knew of the great horrors and plagues the God of Israel brought upon the Egyptians during the time of Moses and the great exodus of the Hebrews.

God needed a priest to bring the Ark of the Covenant to its rightful place in Jerusalem. Did God go get a priest? No, He used His worshiper. King David brought the Ark of the Covenant back to the people of God.

When God Finds a Worshiper

When God finds a true worshiper, He can make that worshiper anything He needs them to be. That's what He's called you and I to do; He has called you and I to worship. The Father can trust a true worshiper. A true worshiper will always have the Father's best interest in his heart. God knows his motives are pure. The Lord knows that His worshiper is going to bring glory to Him and not to man. A true worshiper will not touch God's glory or claim any credit for the things the Father does through him.

CHAPTER 4

WHAT IS PRAISE?

P*raise* by definition is when we recite or declare the acts, deeds, works, character, attributes or promises of God. An example of praise is to say, "God is good. God is great. God is awesome. God is almighty. God is victorious; the battle is the Lord's. He has overcome the enemy."

Whenever someone is going to buy or sell a home, that person will hire a professional to come and examine the property and list all of the assets and points of interest that will make that home attractive to a potential buyer. The appraiser will list things like the area and location of the home. He will give a description of the physical

property which will include things such as:
- Number of bedrooms
- Number of bathrooms
- Number of garage spaces
- Kitchen appliances
- Yard size
- Type of roof
- Type of pool
- Age of the building

This assessment or description of the home is called an appraisal. Every potential buyer or seller will order their own appraisal for this property. Based on the character and attributes of that home, each appraiser will recommend a worth or value. Values will almost always vary because things that are important to one person will not be as important to someone else.

We are the appraisers for God. Based on our experience, knowledge and revelation of Him, we make declarations that describe Him. Each one of us will have some common things and some unique things to say about Him because He has done common and unique things in all of our lives.

Praise can be horizontal or vertical. Praise can be **about** God or **to** God. When we talk about Him to others and make declarations about Him, this is considered **horizontal praise**. For example, when we say "God is great," we are declaring one of the attributes of God to others.

When we say to the Father, "God, you are great," we are speaking directly to Him and that is called **vertical praise**.

Praise does not require intimacy with God. Many people who are not believers or followers of Christ will make declarations and give credit to God because it is obvious that only God can do some things. Many celebrities and talented individuals will often confess that their talent came from God. They make these declarations because they know that some gifts and talents can only come from a divine source.

Singers, athletes, musicians, entertainers and others will often thank God when receiving awards because they feel that somehow only God could have blessed them to reach and achieve the levels of greatness they have acquired. They know that they could not have done what they did on their own.

Just because these people say wonderful things about the Lord does not mean that they are serving the Lord. They say these things because they cannot deny the fact that God has blessed their lives in extraordinary ways. They give God the praise for their God-given talent, but too often their lives do not bring glory to Him.

They may not have a close relationship with the Father; they praise Him from afar. They know what He has done, but they don't know Him. They don't have a close intimate relationship with Him.

In spite of someone's lack of relationship with the Lord, it is still a good thing to give praise to the Lord. The Bible says in the book of Psalms 150:6, *"Let everything that has breath praise the Lord! Praise ye the Lord."* God wants and loves to be honored and praised by saints and sinners alike.

Praise by definition is to give a favorable commendation.
- It is never negative.
- It is used to establish value.
- It esteems the Lord as worthy.

Praise to God is:
- To recite, rehearse, demonstrate, thank or declare the acts, deeds, works, character, attributes or promises of God.
- Act of the will.
  "I will bless the LORD at all times: his praise shall continually be in my mouth (Psalms 34:1)."
- Required of everything that has breath.
  "Let everything that hast breath praise the LORD Praise ye the Lord. Praise ye the Lord (Psalms 150:6)."

CHAPTER 5

WORD STUDY ON PRAISE

Throughout the English translation of the Bible, the word *praise* is used many times. During the translation of the Scriptures, there were several different expressions, both verbal and physical, that were assigned for the word *praise*. The following words and descriptions are examples of the Hebrew's appraisal of God.

Yadah

The essence of **yadah** is to thrust the hands giving thanks and confession. **Yadah** is generally a loud vocal expression confessing the attributes of God. It includes the thrusting of the hands usually in the context of community, much like a modern day pep rally at a school or college before a big game. This type of praise is declared with the understanding that God in involved along with the people giving the praise.

When we give **yadah**-praise, we know that we are not in the battle alone. We praise and give thanks to God because we know that He is greater than all enemies or foes. We are thanking Him because He takes the responsibility and the glory for the victory. **Yadah** means that God is fighting for us; He has forgiven us and His favor is on us.

A great example of **yadah**-praise is found in the twentieth chapter of 2 Chronicles. The three armies of Ammon, Mount Seir and Moab came to wage war against King Jehoshaphat, the King of Judah. Fear had come upon the people because they knew a victory could not be obtained by strength of numbers alone.

King Jehoshaphat was also afraid; however, he knew that the answer to this situation was not in strength and numbers of fighting men or how strong the wall of the city might be, but in the God of Abraham, Isaac and Jacob.

The king declared a fast and began praying. He reminded God that He was the God of heaven who ruled over all kingdoms and nations. The king called on God to remember that He was the God who drove out the inhabitants of the land

and gave it to the descendants of Abraham. He reminded the Lord that they had built a temple and His name was in it. King Jehoshaphat trusted God to divinely intervene on their behalf, judge, and save them from their enemies. 2 Chronicles 20:12 says:

> *O our God, wilt thou not judge them? for we have no might against this great company that cometh against us; neither know we what to do: but our eyes are upon thee.*

As all of the people were standing, the Spirit of the Lord came upon Jahaziel, the Levite. He began to prophesy the Word of the Lord to the congregation which is recorded in 2 Chronicles 20:15-17:

> *Thus saith the Lord unto you, Be not afraid nor dismayed by reason of this great multitude; for the battle is not yours, but God's. Tomorrow go ye down against them: behold, they come up by the cliff of Ziz; and ye shall find them at the end of the brook, before the wilderness of Jeruel. Ye shall not need to fight in this battle: set yourselves, stand ye still, and see the salvation of the Lord with you, O Judah and Jerusalem: fear not, nor be dismayed; tomorrow go out against them: for the Lord will be with you.*

Afterwards, Jehoshophat and all of the people bowed before the Lord and worshiped Him. The next morning the King appointed singers and musicians to go out before the army singing and praising the Lord. 2 Chronicles 20:21 reads,

> *And when he had consulted with the people, he appointed singers unto the Lord, and that should praise the beauty of holiness, as they went out before the army, and to say, Praise the Lord; for his mercy endureth for ever.*

This exercise of praise was known as **yadah**. As the armies of Judah marched forward, they were thrusting their hands in an attitude of confidence and victory knowing that the battle was no longer theirs; the battle was the Lord's. They were thanking God in advance for the victory over their enemies even though they were greatly out numbered.

God responded to their praise and defeated the enemies. 2 Chronicles 20:22-24 reports:

> *And when they began to sing and to praise, the Lord set the ambushments against the children of Ammon, Moab, and mount Seir, which were come against Judah; and they were smitten. For the children of Ammon and Moab stood up against the inhabitants of*

mount Seir, utterly to slay and destroy them: and when they had made an end of the inhabitants of Seir, every one helped to destroy another. And when Judah came toward the watch tower in the wilderness, they looked unto the multitude, and, behold, they were dead bodies fallen to the earth, and none escaped.

In this awesome story, the people of God used praise as a weapon. They thanked God before the battle even began and they declared His works, deeds and promises. They called upon the living God to intervene in this situation which would surely result in their demise without God's help and assistance. They reminded God that they were His children, the descendants of Abraham.

This **yadah**, the thrusting of the hands and shouting the character, attributes, history and promises of God while giving thanks, was all the people of God needed for God to act on their behalf.

Towdah

Towdah means to extend the hands in an expression of thanks. It is also used to thank God for His promises and covenant with His people. When we thank God for something before it happens, it is a type of *towdah*. This act of praise says, "Lord, I thank you that You will supply all my needs." It might further be said, "Lord I thank You that all my children will be saved and serve You."

Towdah is thanking God in spite of the negative circumstances that we may face. *Towdah* is thanking and giving God glory when we cannot see answers to our problems in the natural. However, on the other hand, knowing that there are spiritual agents or angels that are on assignment from God to fight our battles in the heavenly realm before they manifest in the natural.

When my children were small I worked at a local Community College in Northern California. In the evenings when I would come home from work, my boys would rush to me with their hands outstretched to receive me and celebrate my arrival. They could not wait for me to walk through the door so they could run and jump into my arms. I would tickle and wrestle with them. We would laugh and act silly and have crazy fun every evening.

Many evenings I was tired, but I was never too tired to spend precious time with them. Sometimes I would have serious matters to deal with such as bills and night school homework; however, no matter what I had to do, my concerns took a back seat to spending quality and fun time with my boys and my wife.

My boys never worried about things like bills, house repairs, insurance or car maintenance. They knew that their dad was going to take care of all of those things because that is what dads do. If they were not feeling well, they knew that Dad and Mom were going to do whatever was necessary to make everything all right again because that is what parents do.

When they rushed to me at the end of the day with their arms stretched out and jumped into my arms, it was like a type of *towdah*. My promise and responsibility to them is to protect and provide for them in every way. Their outstretched arms reaching out to receive me was a demonstration of their full faith and confidence in me to do all of the things that will make their lives safe and their basic needs supplied.

When we extend our hands and arms to God our Father in the expression of *towdah*, we are saying to Him that we have no worries or fears because He shall supply all of our needs according to His riches in glory by Christ Jesus according to Philippians 4:19. Our extended hands, or *towdah*, are a way of our saying to our Father that our full faith and confidence is in Him and we will not be afraid or shaken by anything that may try to steal our joy. We are letting Him know that we are not worried about the many things that try to disturb our composure. We are telling God that we know He is ready, willing and able to take care of us. Our **towdah** is a way of saying thanks to our Father and declaring that all is well because of Him.

A scriptural example of **towdah** is found in Psalms 50:23, *"Whoever offereth praise glorifieth me: and to him that ordereth his conversation aright will I shew the salvation of God."*

Shabach

Shabach is a shout to God. Shouting to God with a loud voice helps us release our emotions and find freedom in the spirit. Generally, when we shout, we throw off all of our inhibitions and reservations and release ourselves to the excitement of the moment. We don't care who is watching or what anyone thinks about us. It's great when others share in our joy and celebration, but if they don't join with us, we refuse to let their nonparticipation steal our joy.

During most of the time that I served in the United States Air Force, I was involved in the Air Force talent contest. Each year at our base, a contest would be held for airmen who were talented in the entertainment arts. There were many categories such as: male vocalist, female vocalist, bands, vocal groups, dancers and comedians.

There were many stages of the contests: local, regional, national and worldwide. Everyone began at the local level and those who won continued to rise to the next level until the worldwide winners had been chosen. Every year I was blessed to win at several levels. My greatest joy was competing at the worldwide level as a solo male artist in which I finished third place. Each level of competition brought its own stress and intimidation. Every competition was filled with extremely talented individuals.

Whenever the judges would announce the point totals and the winners, there would be uncontrollable jubilation and victory shouts. For the winners, those were moments that will forever live in their hearts and minds. Personally, I have never lost my voice from singing, but on many occasions I lost my voice as a result of the unbridled shouting and celebrating at the parties we had after I had been declared a winner.

Those were wonderful times in my life; however, they do not compare to the ongoing celebration of my life since I committed my life to the Lord Jesus. I don't try to win trophies and awards anymore. My greatest passion is winning souls. Each time my ministry team and I present a praise concert, it is my prayer that lost souls come into the Kingdom of God

There are shouts of joy at each meeting when sinners become saints after praying the prayer of faith with me. I always invite the congregation to join the band and I when we release ourselves to shout to the Lord for the great miracle He has done. When a person is born again into the Kingdom, all of heaven is rejoicing along with those of us here on earth.

When we praise the Lord with a loud voice for the things He has done or for who He is, we have exercised a **shabach**. The following Scriptures are examples of **shabach**:

> Because thy loving kindness is better than life, my lips shall praise thee (Psalms 63:3).

> O praise the Lord, all you nations: praise him, all ye people (Psalms 117:1).

> Praise the LORD, O Jerusalem; praise thy God, O Zion (Psalms 147:12).

> One generation shall praise thy works to another, and shall declare thy mighty acts (Psalms 145:4).

> And say ye, Save us, O God of our salvation, and gather us together, and deliver us from the heathen, that we may give thanks to thy holy name, and glory in thy praise (1 Chronicles 16:35).

Save us, O LORD our God, and gather us from among the heathen, to give thanks unto thy holy name, and to triumph in thy praise (Psalms 106:47).

And when he was come nigh, even now at the descent of the mount of Olives, the whole multitude of the disciples began to rejoice and praise God with a loud voice for all the mighty works that they had seen; Saying, Blessed be the King that cometh in the name of the Lord: peace in heaven, and glory in the highest (Luke 19: 37-38).

People who **shabach** are often criticized. Some consider this type of worship as undignified especially those people who are uptight and full of pride. People who are uncomfortable with loud praise are more concerned about what others think of them than what God thinks of them.

When our Lord Jesus made His triumphant entry into the city of Jerusalem on a donkey, a multitude of followers came out to meet Him shouting *hosanna*. Some of the religious leaders wanted Jesus to rebuke the people and quiet their shouting. Jesus, on the other hand, encouraged the people and rebuked the Pharisees and told them that if the people did not praise Him then the rocks would cry out in their place. This is recorded in Luke 19:39-40 which says:

And some of the Pharisees from among the multitude said unto him, Master, rebuke thy disciples. And he answered and said unto them, I tell you that, if these should hold their peace, the stones would immediately cry out.

I love to shout out to the Lord both in celebration and petition. When I shout in celebration I know that the angelic hosts are celebrating with me. Jesus prayed, *"Your will be done on earth as it is in Heaven (Luke 11:2)."* With every account of a heavenly experience in Scripture, there is loud and intense praise and worship around the throne of God. He has chosen to make his habitation in us and in order to be consistent with the heavenly realms, I find it appropriate to release my praise in a continuous manner like King David encouraged us to do. We read King David's words in Psalms 34:1, *"I will bless the Lord at all times and His praise will continually be in my mouth."* I don't want a rock to replace me at praising my Lord. I refuse to let a rock or anything else replace my praise.

Zamar

Zamar is to make music or play on instruments. This is the Hebrew word for praising God through singing or playing on musical instruments. In Psalm 150, the writer gives a command to the musicians and singers to praise the Lord with all of the instruments and voices. The writer, probably King David, commanded that the Lord must be praised in the heavens and the sanctuary. We are instructed to praise Him for His mighty works, deeds and excellent greatness.

Every instrument is required to praise the Lord with enthusiasm and high energy. No instrument is exempt from offering praise. The same is true for today. We should use every tool available to establish His glory and greatness.

In this age of technology, we have many more musical instruments than the people had in the times when the Psalms were written. Not only do we have more instruments, but we have electrical modifications to amplify and add color and variation to the sound of the instruments. We even have visual effects that can be added to the music as it is being performed. Words and photos can be reflected on a screen making it easier for all to read as the music is played.

With words and song books so readily available, there is absolutely no reason for anyone to have an excuse for not praising the Lord. Every voice is required to be filled with the glorious praise of our great God.

Psalms 150

Praise ye the Lord. Praise God in his sanctuary: praise him in the firmament of his power. Praise him for his mighty acts: praise him according to his excellent greatness. Praise him with the sound of the trumpet: praise him with the psaltery and harp. Praise him with the timbrel and dance: praise him with stringed instruments and organs. Praise him upon the loud cymbals: praise him upon the high sounding cymbals. Let every thing that hath breath praise the Lord. Praise ye the Lord.

Halal

Halal means to rave, boast, celebrate, jump and shine. **Halal** is the root word for *hallelujah*. *Hallelujah* or *alleluia* is used all over the world as an expression of praise to the Lord. It is used as a way of exalting the name of the Lord. *Hallelujah* is spoken loudly or when it is spoken softly, it is spoken with passion and intensity. This word is used to commend God the Father and magnify or boast about His great works and deeds.

One of the definitions of *halal* is to be clamorously foolish. The Hebrew people worshiped and praised a God that no one could see. All of the other nations worshiped an object that had been made by man's hands or something in nature that they could see and identify. They worshiped the sun, moon, objects in nature, animals or other creatures that could not answer them nor meet their needs.

Jehovah, the God of the Hebrews, on the other hand, not only answered their prayers, but He visited them with His manifested presence as a response to the appropriate praise and worship of His people. He was a God who talked to His people and gave them specific laws and instructions. Jehovah went before them in battle and gave them miraculous victories. The Hebrew God brought shame and destruction to the other so-called gods of the other nations.

Because no one could see the Hebrew God, other nations could easily call the Hebrews foolish when they praised and exalted their God; that is until they had been touched or destroyed by he wrath of the God of Abraham, Isaac and Jacob.

When the Hebrews praised their God, they threw off their inhibitions and celebrated with fervor and excitement. Why not boast about their great God? Jehovah had delivered them, fed them, protected them, prospered them and fought for them. He had brought them into a land that had cities they did not build, vineyards they did not plant, and wells they did not dig. He had fulfilled His promise to their ancestors and made promises to them that He would always be with them if they obeyed His word and commandments.

Why not shout? They had something to shout about! Why not dance and sing? They had reasons to dance and sing! When they looked at all He had done for them and all He planned to do, it should have been easy for them to love, thank and boast about Him. He was their God and they were His chosen people.

I am a sports fan. I really enjoy my favorite teams. They bring me joy and excitement especially when they win a title or a championship. I celebrate with them when they win the big game. I jump, yell, scream and act silly and foolish with high fives and low fives when they win a championship or a world title. Unfortunately amusement is all I get from being one of their fans. They get prestige and huge salaries and I'm all for that; but, all I get from being a supporter is a few hours of fun and sometimes a hoarse voice.

Jesus is my champion. He has won more than just a title. He has won the world! He has won the victory of all victories. He is the champion of all champions. He holds all of the records and there are no more games to be played.

Unlike my sports heroes, He has shared the rewards of victory with me and others who believe in Him. We are more than conquerors because the victory He won was not for Himself; it was for all of those who follow Him and keep His commandments. It was for all who are filled with His Spirit and doing His will. Because of His victory, we have abundant and eternal life. We have access and an audience with God our Father. We have peace, joy and pleasures forevermore.

That is why we praise Him. That's why we boast, shout, dance and celebrate before Him. He Himself has invited us to sing out loud and play on the instruments before Him. He has invited us to make a joyful noise before Him. God loves praise and I love to praise Him. He is and has always been all of the wonderful and awesome things we declare that He is. God is good and His mercy is everlasting.

I am not ashamed of who and what He is. If I look foolish praising my Savior, then I will continue to look foolish. If my praise makes the hypocrite uncomfortable, so be it. If my dancing before the Lord causes me to seem undignified then I'll just have to wear that label. I would rather find favor in the eyes of God than try to satisfy the hearts of men.

I celebrate Him because I know what He has done for me. I can't argue or discuss what He has done or not done for others. I just know what He has done for me and my family. I'm very proud of my God. His praise will forever be in my mouth.

Tehillah

Tehillah means the praise that God inhabits. The Bible says in Psalms 22:3, *"But thou art holy, O thou that inhabitest the praises of Israel."* Let us examine this verse in detail.

Holy means that God is separate and set apart. In order to be holy is to be pure and un-contaminated - without blemish and incorrupt-ible. *Inhabit* means to dwell in or be enthroned upon. *Praises* are a favorable commendation.

Is it any wonder that King David worshiped God? He said in Psalms 34:1, *"I will bless the Lord at all times. His praise will continually be in my mouth."* King David had revelations and in-sights about the Father that were far beyond the people of his time. He knew that if he continually lifted up the names and attributes of God, then God was committed to respond to David's confes-sions and declarations.

- David declared God to be his Shepherd - God had to Shepherd him (Psalms 23:1).
- David declared God to be his Shield - God had to protect him (Psalms 3:3).
- David declared God his King and Lord - God had to be his authority and source (Psalms 5:2).
- David trusted God for salvation - God had to save him (Psalms 7:1).

God and His Word are one. When He speaks something, it must come to pass. If He said He will do a certain thing, He will do it. That is the reason why it is so important to know and pray God's Word. He is the Word; He cannot change. He must fulfill His Word. He watches over His Word to perform it.

When we pray and declare His promises and recite His character in faith and trust, God has to respond to that declaration because He dwells in those expressions of favorable commendation. He inhabits our praises. He lives in our praises.

How can we have the assurance that God is always with us? Praise Him. In the midst of difficult situations, keep praising God. When we pray the prayer of faith and declare that Jesus is Lord of our lives, we immediately receive salvation. That same faith and declaration that saved us is the same faith and declaration that will deliver us from the issues that challenge us on a daily basis. The presence of God is as near to you as your words of praise.

- Call Him your Savior and He will be there to save you.
- Call Him your peace and He is there to give you peace that passes all understanding.
- Call Him your provider and know that He shall provide for all your needs according to His riches in glory by Christ Jesus.
- Call Him your King and His righteousness separates you from sins you've committed.
- Call Him your Lord and He immediately takes responsibility for your welfare and care.
- Call Him your defense and He becomes your advocate.

- Call Him at any place because He will never leave you or forsake you.
- Call Him anytime because He never slumbers or sleeps.
- Call on His name because His very name means salvation.

HE INHABITS OUR PRAISE - Tehillah.

CHAPTER 6

WHAT IS WORSHIP?

I believe that worship is a matter of the heart. You can have the best band, the best dancers, the best banners, but if there is not heart involvement, you have nothing more than a show

Acts of worship include:

- to kneel
- to bow
- to pay tribute
- to reverence
- to serve
- to lay prostrate

First and foremost, worship is the only appropriate act of behavior in the presence of royalty or deity. It is the avenue to the heart of God; worship requires faith. Anyone who comes to God must believe that He exists and He rewards those who diligently seek Him. Our acts of worship to God are not only gestures of respect to Him, but they are also a demonstration of our adoration and gratitude toward the One who created us and sustains us.

There is no substitute for worship. Although many refuse to worship the Lord appropriately in this life, it is important to know that there will come a day when every knee in heaven, on the earth and under the earth will bow and every tongue will confess that Jesus Christ is Lord to the glory of God. Philippians 2:9-11 says,

> *Wherefore God also hath highly exalted him, and given him a name which is above every name: that at the name of Jesus every knee should bow, of things in heaven, and things in earth, and things under the earth; and that every tongue should confess that Jesus Christ is Lord, to the glory of God the Father.*

Worship is Always Vertical

Worship should always be directed to God as if we were talking to Him face to face. Praise, of course, can be horizontal or vertical, but worship is always directed vertically to God. A very popular worship song in churches today is entitled "I Love You, Lord." This song is a love song to God and is sung with deep heartfelt passion. It is a song that causes the singer or worshiper to become intimate with God.

True worship requires intimacy with God. The closer we are to Him, the more intense our worship becomes. When we draw near to Him, He will draw near to us. The more we desire Him, the more He reveals Himself to us. The purpose for worship is to create an environment for God to manifest His presence. God is faithful to manifest His presence over and over again according to the condition of the worship environment that we create for Him.

God wants to dwell among us. Earlier in this book, I made the statement that the optimum place for man is in the presence of God. In His presence there is fullness of joy and pleasures forever more. In His presence there is eternal life. Death is defined as separation from God. There is life, and life abundantly, wherever God is found. Jesus came that we might have life abundantly. God wants to be with us.

> *For God so loved the world, that he gave*
> *his only begotten Son, that whosoever*
> *believeth in him should not perish, but*

have everlasting life. For God sent not his Son into the world to condemn the world; but that the world through him might be saved. He that believeth on him is not condemned: but he that believeth not is condemned already, because he hath not believed in the name of the only begotten Son of God. And this is the condemnation, that light is come into the world, and men loved darkness rather than light, because their deeds were evil. For every one that doeth evil hateth the light, neither cometh to the light, lest his deeds should be reproved. But he that doeth truth cometh to the light, that his deeds may be made manifest, that they are wrought in God (John 3:16-21).

1 John 1:5-7 reads:

This then is the message which we have heard of him, and declare unto you, that God is light, and in him is no darkness at all. 6 If we say that we have fellowship with him, and walk in darkness, we lie, and do not the truth: but if we walk in the light, as he is in the light, we have fellowship one with another, and the blood of Jesus Christ his Son cleanseth us from all sin.

It is recorded in John 1:1-9 that:

> *In the beginning was the Word, and the Word was with God, and the Word was God. The same was in the beginning with God. All things were made by him; and without him was not any thing made that was made. In him was life; and the life was the light of men. And the light shineth in darkness; and the darkness comprehended it not. There was a man sent from God, whose name was John. The same came for a witness, to bear witness of the Light, that all men through him might believe. He was not that Light, but was sent to bear witness of that Light. That was the true Light, which lighteth every man that cometh into the world.*

True Worship Begins in the Heart

True worship is more than the lovely songs we sing in our church services. True worship is more than the poetic phrases and melodies that make us cry and give us chill bumps when we sing them. It is more than the awesome feelings we get when we fellowship with each other at corporate gatherings.

True worship begins in the heart and manifests in emotions and actions that are signs or evidence that God is with us. The Word says, *"Out of the abundance of the heart the mouth speaketh (Matthew 12:34)."* If we love God, our gratitude will come out of our mouths.

When we are happy, we sing happy songs like "Happy Birthday." When we are sad, we sing the blues. When we celebrate, we sing songs of celebration.

When we are in love, we sing love songs. We demonstrate our commitment to God by singing songs of worship and adoration. The attitudes and feelings in our hearts will come out of our mouths in expressions of love and admiration to the Father. Don't think that I have something against crying or being broken in spirit; just the opposite is true. Very often when I worship my Father God, I find myself getting mushy and watery-eyed. I know how much He loves me and I know how much I don't deserve the love He has given to me, except by the blood of His marvelous Son, Jesus.

My heart is so full of love for the Lord that I have dedicated to Him all that I am and all that I ever hope to become. The Father is looking past the outward appearances of people. He is looking deep down inside our hearts. He can see if there are any hidden motives in our relationship with

Him; He can tell if our agendas are inconsistent with His. The Lord knows exactly what we are all about. 1 Samuel 16:7 says,

> *But the Lord said unto Samuel, Look not on his countenance, or on the height of his stature; because I have refused him: for the Lord seeth not as man seeth; for man looketh on the outward appearance, but the Lord looketh on the heart.*

Other Words for *Worship*

There are several words used in Scripture that are interchangeable with the word *worship*. It is important when you see these words to know that it could be worship or be directly associated with the word *worship*.

- To serve
- To offer gifts
- To perform sacred services
- To minister to
- To kiss
- To reverence
- To kneel
- To wait upon
- To lay prostrate
- To bow

I was fortunate and blessed to be in England during the celebration of Queen Elizabeth's fiftieth year on the throne as the reigning monarch. Being an American, it was difficult for me to fully appreciate the depth and magnitude of the celebration. America was founded as a result of a rebellion from a tyrannical British King. Because Americans have never had a royal family, it is hard for us to understand the appropriate etiquette and protocol in the presence of royalty.

Growing up and living in America, we were never taught how to appreciate and serve royal personalities. In the United States, we have elected officials. The people choose mayors, governors, congressmen, senators and presidents. We are not required to serve or wait on them and we do not have to bow before them. They take an oath to serve the people and are accountable to the people for a limited amount of years.

To bow before someone is to declare that they are the greater and you are the lesser. In America, our constitution declares that we are all created equal. There is no greater or lesser. Citizens of the United States are not conditioned or programmed for bowing, kneeling and serving.

In most of the nations that our ministry has visited around the world, these gestures of honor and respect are common. Royalty deserves honor and reverence. Many people in the western hemisphere find it really hard to worship King Jesus because they have never been taught how to honor and revere a king. Jesus is a king. In fact He is the King of Kings. Wise men worship Him and they bow, serve, wait on Him and pay tribute to Him.

The apostle Paul even tells us to present our bodies as living sacrifices to God which is our reasonable service. He made this admonition in Romans 12:1-2:

> *I beseech you therefore, brethren, by the mercies of God, that ye present your bodies a living sacrifice, holy, acceptable unto God, which is your reasonable service. And be not conformed to this world: but be ye transformed by the renewing of your mind, that ye may prove what is that good, and acceptable, and perfect, will of God.*

CHAPTER 7

BALANCED
WITH THE WORD

Our praise and worship experiences must be balanced with the Word of God. The words to songs must be scriptural and in proper Biblical context. Many songs that traffic in the Body of Christ are not in line with what the Word of God teaches us. When we teach our congregations to sing these songs, we are endorsing error.

The Bible tells us in 2 Timothy 2:15, *"Study to show thyself approved unto God, a worker that needeth not to be ashamed, rightly dividing the word of truth."*

Every song that we teach our congregations should be studied lyrically. It is the leader's responsibility to ensure they are not teaching error to the people. The songs may be popular and have great hook lines and catch phrases, but if they don't match the Word of God they need to be changed or thrown out. Pastors should not have to apologize for inaccuracies that have been written in songs and accepted by publishing companies and recording companies who are more interested in selling music than being accurate in the Word.

I thank God for the abundance of music that the church receives from the many recording companies in America and around the world. Overall, these companies have helped the church world come into a new era of corporate praise and worship. They have helped thousands of congregations lay down their hymn books and enter into a new level of celebration.

On the other hand, much of the music that is used in the church is not accomplishing its purpose. Today, there are many songs that God cannot receive as worship in truth. True worship requires accuracy, knowledge and understanding.

The Offering of Cain

When we try to worship the Father with song lyrics that do not reflect the Word of God in context and accuracy, it can be compared to the offerings that Cain offered to God in Genesis chapter three. Cain's offering was unacceptable to God because it did not satisfy the requirements that God had established with his parents, Adam and Eve.

When Adam and Eve sinned in the Garden of Eden, God expelled them from the Garden and clothed them with animal skins. This is recorded in Genesis 3:20-21, *"And Adam called his wife's name Eve; because she was the mother of all living. Unto Adam also and to his wife did the Lord God make coats of skins, and clothed them."*

God made clothes from the skins of animals and covered them. A principle was established that set the pattern for God to forgive sin: an innocent animal had to die in order for sin to be atoned or covered.

We see in Leviticus 17:11, *"For the life of the flesh is in the blood: and I have given it to you upon the altar to make an atonement for your souls: for it is the blood that maketh an atonement for the soul."*

Cain sacrificed a grain offering from his fields and it was unacceptable to God. The Bible does not say if Cain was sincere in his giving or not, but it clearly states that God was not pleased. Cain planted his fields. He took the time to prepare an altar, gathered his gift and presented it before God. He made a genuine effort to give an offering, but God was not pleased with what he presented.

The offerings that we present before God must be according to God's instructions. Jesus tells us in John 4 that God is seeking worship in spirit and truth. Cain wanted to worship, but he wanted to do it his way. We are instructed to worship in spirit (with a pure heart, sincere, desire to please) but we are also instructed to worship in truth (knowledge and understanding). There is a right way and a wrong way to present offerings to the Father.

If we come before Him singing songs that do not accurately depict the nature and character of God or violate the teachings that He has given to us in His Word, we are no better than Cain. We cannot expect God to honor these sacrifices of praise. In fact, we insult Him when we say or sing things about Him that He did not say or do. If we sing or make up clever sounding poetic phrases that make people feel good but are not in line with what the Bible says, we are in danger of losing the favor of God.

Sincerely Wrong

The great King David is celebrated as our primary example of a worshiper. He wrote many of the songs of praise and worship in the book of Psalms. Many of our praise and worship patterns were established in David's service to the Lord. God honored him and exalted him because he was a man after God's heart.

No one ever questioned David's sincerity about worshiping God. He was and still is a great role model for all who love and trust in the Lord. In the good times, he praised the Lord. In the bad times, he continued to praise and worship the God of Israel. He lived a life of worship and praise.

David was a true worshiper. God allowed him to be the one to usher the Ark of the Covenant, which represented God's presence, back to its proper place among the people of Israel. This responsibility had been given to the priests of the tribe of Levi by way of the covenant which God Himself established with Moses in the Sinai Desert. David was not a Levite; he was a descendant of the tribe of Judah. Under normal circumstances, his family lineage alone disqualified David from having any participation in matters that concerned the Ark of the Covenant or the Tabernacle of Moses.

The Ark of the Covenant had been ignored for more than twenty years. King David had a passion for the presence of God. He organized a processional to escort the Ark to Jerusalem with music, sacrifices and dancing. When the oxen stumbled and it appeared that the Ark was going to fall over, a young man named Uzzah reached out and touched the Ark and he died as a result.

The mishandling of the Ark cost a man his life. Of course, this upset the King. This incident caused David to reevaluate his motives and methods. It caused him to study the Levitical writings and seek counsel from the Lord. After studying the Word of the Lord, he learned that the right way to carry the Ark was with poles carried on the shoulders of the priests.

King David's second attempt to deliver the Ark of God to Jerusalem was successful. The processional involved the same type of excitement as the first attempt. There was dancing, singing, sacrifices, and celebration, but this effort was carried out according to the instructions that God had given in the beginning.

David was sincere in both attempts to carry the Ark; however, sincerity alone is not enough in the presence of God. God is holy and He will protect His holiness at all costs. Many times we may mean well or intend to do good things, but in matters that involve the presence of God sincerity and good intentions are not enough. We must act according to God's prescribed plan. It is easy to be sincere, but we can be sincerely wrong at the same time.

In our modern day attempts to worship the Father, we must remember that God does not change. We must always be aware that we cannot bring God anything we feel like bringing Him and think He is going to accept it. We cannot present to God anything that is unacceptable in His sight. Like He did to Cain, God will reject you and your offerings, too.

We can be as sincere as King David in his first attempt to deliver the Ark and be sincerely wrong. God is not a respecter of persons. The Lord rejected David's first attempt to deliver the Ark because David did not follow the written instructions that had been given to the priests. God brought correction to David and he will not spare us from His correction if we choose to ignore His written Word in our efforts to praise and worship Him. We cannot treat His presence lightly. He deserves the best praise and worship that we can give and He will not settle for less.

God is a God of order and design. Divine order is part of the character of God. He wants all things to be done decently, in order and according to His Word.

CHAPTER 8

SONGS OF WORSHIP

The songs that we sing in our corporate worship are important to our worship gatherings. They help us to be in unity and there is strength in unity. In Psalms 133:1-3, we see how anointing and unity are directly related to each other:

> *Behold, how good and how pleasant it is for brethren to dwell together in unity! It is like the precious ointment upon the head, that ran down upon the beard, even Aaron's beard: that went down to the skirts of his garments; As the dew of Hermon, and as the dew that descended upon the mountains of Zion: for there*

*the Lord commanded the blessing, even
life for evermore.*

It is good and pleasant for the people of
God to be in unity and harmony in all things. One
can put a thousand to flight; two can put ten
thousands to flight. It is always to our advantage
to work towards standing with others. We can do
so much more together and in unity than when
we stand alone. The oil being poured over Aaron's
head represents anointing or being set apart to do
a certain work. We have a certain great work to
do and we have been given this task by our Savior to take the gospel to the world. To do this
properly, we need empowerment from on high.

When the priests were together singing during the dedication of King Solomon's Temple, the
presence of the Lord filled the room. When the
disciples gathered in the upper room, the Holy
Spirit came and fell upon them and they began to
speak in unknown tongues.

God loves music and He loves to have His
children together as one. He loves to see His children together, singing before Him and worshiping
Him.

The songs we sing help us to remember the
great works and deed He has done for us. Songs
help us remember His majesty and lordship. Our
songs to Him help us remember His great mercy

and steadfast love for us. Our songs help us re-member the plans that He has for our future.

Our songs must be a reflection of His Word.

- His Word is a lamp.
  Psalms 119:105, *"Thy word is a lamp unto my feet, and a light unto my path."*

- His Word is truth.
  John 17:17-19, *"Sanctify them through thy truth: thy word is truth. As thou hast sent me into the world, even so have I also sent them into the world. And for their sakes I sanctify myself, that they also might be sanctified through the truth."*

- God is one with His word.
  John 1:1, *"In the beginning was the Word, and the Word was with God, and the Word was God."*

Our songs must bring light

- God is light and in Him there is no darkness.

  This then is the message which we have heard of him, and declare unto you, that God is light, and in him is no darkness at all. If we say that we have fellowship with him, and walk in darkness, we lie, and do not the truth: but if we walk in the light, as he is in the light, we have fellowship one with another, and the blood of Jesus Christ his Son cleanseth us from all sin (1 John 1:5-7).

- He has brought us out of darkness and into His marvelous light.
  John 1:8-9, *"He was not that Light, but was sent to bear witness of that Light. That was the true Light, which lighteth every man that cometh into the world."*

- Jesus is the Light of the world.
  John 8:12, *"Then spake Jesus again unto them, saying, I am the light of the world: he that followeth me shall not walk in darkness, but shall have the light of life."*

Our songs must bring revelation.

- He will teach us His ways.

  But the Comforter, which is the Holy Ghost, whom the Father will send in my name, he shall teach you all things, and bring all things to your remembrance, whatsoever I have said unto you (John 14:26).

- He will guide us.
  Psalms 48:14, *"For this God is our God for*

*ever and ever: he will be our guide even
unto death."*

*Howbeit when he, the Spirit of truth, is
come, he will guide you into all truth: for
he shall not speak of himself; but whatsoever he shall hear, that shall he speak:
and he will shew you things to come
(John 16:13).*

• He will show us His rewards.

*But as it is written, Eye hath not seen,
nor ear heard, neither have entered into
the heart of man, the things which God
hath prepared for them that love him.
But God hath revealed them unto us by
his Spirit: for the Spirit searcheth all
things, yea, the deep things of God. For
what man knoweth the things of a man,
save the spirit of man which is in him?
even so the things of God knoweth no
man, but the Spirit of God (1 Corinthians 2:9-11).*

John 15:7, *"If ye abide in me, and my words
abide in you, ye shall ask what ye will, and it
shall be done unto you."*

Our songs must bring hope.

- Christ in us the hope of glory.
  Colossians 1:27, *"To whom God would make known what is the riches of the glory of this mystery among the Gentiles; which is Christ in you, the hope of glory."*

- He is the subject of our faith.
  Hebrews 11:1, *"Now faith is the substance of things hoped for, the evidence of things not seen."*

- Hope does not disappoint.
  Romans 5:5, *"And hope maketh not ashamed; because the love of God is shed abroad in our hearts by the Holy Ghost which is given unto us".*

Our songs must bring glory to the Father, Son and Holy Spirit.

- Glory belongs to God.

  If any man speak, let him speak as the oracles of God; if any man minister, let him do it as of the ability which God giveth: that God in all things may be glorified through Jesus Christ, to whom be praise and dominion for ever and ever. Amen (1 Peter 4:11).

- We beheld His glory.
  John 1:14, *And the Word was made flesh,*

and dwelt among us, (and we beheld his glory, the glory as of the only begotten of the Father,) full of grace and truth."

- The angels give glory to God.

And suddenly there was with the angel a multitude of the heavenly host praising God, and saying, Glory to God in the highest, and on earth peace, good will toward men (Luke 2:13-14).

CHAPTER 9

WORSHIP OR WORK

I t is recorded in Luke 10:38-42:

Now it came to pass, as they went, that he entered into a certain village: and a certain woman named Martha received him into her house. And she had a sister called Mary, which also sat at Jesus' feet, and heard his word. But Martha was cumbered about much serving, and came to him, and said, Lord, dost thou not care that my sister hath left me to serve alone? bid her therefore that she help me. And Jesus answered and said unto her, Martha, Martha, thou art careful and troubled about many things: but one thing is needful: and Mary hath chosen that good part, which shall not be taken away from her.

Work is important and good, but intimacy with the Lord is much more important. I have worked very hard throughout my life. By the grace of God, I have provided well for my family over the years. They love and appreciate my work ethic and the way that I have made sure that they have not been denied anything they have needed and most of the desires of their heart. My wife has an excellent car to drive. She has many classy and expensive clothes for every occasion. She has money to spend on herself and give to others; she loves our home and she feels safe and comfortable in it.

All of these things are wonderful and special, but more than anything she wants and needs to be close and intimate with me. I can do all kinds of things for her and take her to fancy places, but nothing takes the place of me putting my arms around her and telling her that I love her. Nothing can take the place of me looking into her eyes and reassuring her of my commitment and devotion to our marriage. It's wonderful that we have lots of beautiful things now; but, it was when we had hardly any material wealth at all that our love for each other was enough to keep us going.

I work very hard and do my best to do all of the things that I am responsible to do. I am generous and reasonably thoughtful. I genuinely love being a blessing to my wife. With all of my giving and taking, coming and going, the best part of our relationship is our talking and touching. Intimacy is the key to a loving relationship. Work is good and necessary, but intimacy is the maintenance element that keeps a loving relationship strong and lasting.

Intimacy with the Lord is what keeps our relationship with Him strong and lasting. He wants to give us many things, but more than anything He wants us to be close and personal with Him. He wants us to be able to hear and recognize His voice and not be distracted by another voice. Jesus said in John 10 that He is the good Shepherd and His sheep know His voice and will not follow another. We must develop an intimate and close relationship with Him to enable us to distinguish His voice in the midst of any chaos, confusion or any other thing that would attempt to draw us away from Him.

Mary knew and understood the importance of being at the feet of Jesus. Somehow she knew that being close to Him and hearing what He had to say was important. Mary was not going to let this special moment and opportunity escape or pass her by. Mary anointed the feet of Jesus with precious oil and dried His feet with her hair. In her heart, she knew that this was more important to Jesus than the work that Martha was doing.

Martha was ministering **for** the Lord; Mary was ministering **to** the Lord. Both of these ministries are important, but Jesus Himself declared that Mary had chosen the better ministry. Quite often, people will work very hard for the Kingdom of God. They will spend hours and hours doing things that really need to be done, but somehow they never find the time to minister to the Lord. The Father wants us to spend precious and intimate time with Him.

Some of the disciples, Judas in particular, rebuked Mary for ministering to Jesus the way she was attending to Him. Judas accused her of wasting very precious and expensive oil. Jesus, on the other hand, rebuked Judas, who was a thief anyway, and acknowledged that this was a special moment for Mary. She had saved this expensive oil especially for the Savior, and the moment had come for her to pour out this tangible expression of her love on the Lord's body. Jesus protected her in her act of worship.

Ministry for the Lord vs. Ministry to the Lord

In the seventh chapter of Matthew, Jesus talks about those who will come to Him on the Day of Judgment and talk about the good things they have done in His name. Doing good works is not a substitute for knowing or having an intimate or personal relationship with Him. God had gone to great lengths to be among us and have fellowship with us. We must get our priorities right. Knowing Him and spending quality time with Him is the best thing we can do in our worship experience. Matthew 7:21-23 records:

> *Not every one that saith unto me, Lord, Lord, shall enter into the kingdom of heaven; but he that doeth the will of my Father which is in heaven. Many will say to me in that day, Lord, Lord, have we not prophesied in thy name? and in thy name have cast out devils? and in thy name done many wonderful works? And then will I profess unto them, I never knew you: depart from me, ye that work iniquity.*

What a great disappointment it will be on the Day of Judgment for many people when the Lord will reject those who did great works, but had no genuine relationship with Him. We get to know the Lord in our time of close and intimate fellowship with Him. It is worship that takes us to the heart of God. It is through worship that we know the heart of God. It is through worship that we receive wisdom and understanding from God. It is through worship that we get our assignments and commissions from God. Isaiah wrote:

In the year that king Uzziah died I saw also the Lord sitting upon a throne, high and lifted up, and his train filled the temple. Above it stood the seraphims: each one had six wings; with twain he covered his face, and with twain he covered his feet, and with twain he did fly. And one cried unto another, and said, Holy, holy, holy, is the Lord of hosts: the whole earth is full of his glory. And the posts of the door moved at the voice of him that cried, and the house was filled with smoke. Then said I, Woe is me! for I am undone; because I am a man of unclean lips, and I dwell in the midst of a people of unclean lips: for mine eyes have seen the King, the Lord of hosts. Then flew one of the seraphims unto me, having a live coal in his hand, which he had taken with the tongs from off the altar: and he laid it upon my mouth, and said, Lo, this hath touched thy lips; and thine iniquity is taken away, and thy sin purged. Also I heard the voice of the Lord, saying, Whom shall I send, and who will go for us? Then said I, Here am I; send me. And he said, Go, and tell this people, Hear ye indeed, but understand not; and see ye indeed, but perceive not. Make the heart of this people fat, and make their ears heavy, and shut their eyes; lest they see with their eyes, and

hear with their ears, and understand
with their heart, and convert, and be
healed (Isaiah 6:1-10).

Yes, work is good, but it is when we spend
time with the Lord that we get instructions for
the work He wants done. We get our assignments
and mandates in our intimate times with Him.
The Lord will give us dreams, visions and revelations of what is on His heart and what He wants
us to do. It is during those intimate times with
Him that He prepares us for the assignments He
has for us.

It is when we worship Him in spirit and
truth that He gets our full and undivided attention. He wants all of our attention when we come
before Him. When we make His agenda our
agenda, we make ourselves eligible for His trust.
When we cast down our own motives and ambi-
tions and make God's desires the desires of our
hearts, He will reveal the plans that He has for us.
When we do the will of the Father, He is then glorified. When we live a life of continuous worship,
His words will always be in our hearts and in our
mouths. Whatever we ask the Father, He will do it
for us because His will has become our will and our
desire is to do His will on the earth just as His will
is done in Heaven.

John 15:7-8 says:

*If ye abide in me, and my words abide in
you, ye shall ask what ye will, and it shall
be done unto you. Herein is my Father glorified, that ye bear much fruit; so shall ye
be my disciples.*

Too many people think they can impress
God with works alone. Many people will do things
in the name of the Lord that the Lord never told
them to do. Some of those works may be good
works in our own eyes, but God is only pleased
when we do what He has instructed us to do. True
worship requires knowing the Word of the Lord
and obeying His commands.

King Saul lost his favor with God because
he was disobedient to the Word of the Lord. In
His arrogance and pride, he disobeyed God and
pretended he was doing Him a favor. The Lord
does not need our favors. God wants us to learn
and follow His commands and instructions. God
is God all by Himself. The Lord does not need us
to make decisions for Him. He knows the end of
things before they begin. It is recorded in 1 Samuel
13:11-14:

*And Samuel said, What hast thou done?
And Saul said, Because I saw that the
people were scattered from me, and that
thou camest not within the days appointed, and that the Philistines gathered themselves together at Michmash;*

therefore said I, The Philistines will come down now upon me to Gilgal, and I have not made supplication unto the Lord: I forced myself therefore, and offered a burnt offering. And Samuel said to Saul, Thou hast done foolishly: thou hast not kept the commandment of the Lord thy God, which he commanded thee: for now would the Lord have established thy kingdom upon Israel for ever. But now thy kingdom shall not continue: the Lord hath sought him a man after his own heart, and the Lord hath commanded him to be captain over his people, because thou hast not kept that which the Lord commanded thee.

When we follow God's plan, He will always get the glory and He will give us the rewards. When we fail to follow His instructions, we have chosen to travel down a road of disappointment that leads ultimately to destruction.

CHAPTER 10

NEW TESTAMENT WORSHIP

In the Old Testament, we get a picture of the many rituals that were involved in the act of worship. There was slaughter of animals, washings, lighting candles, burning incense and making atonements. However, Jesus in His dialogue with the woman at the well in Samaria, instituted a new way of worship for the new covenant believer. True worshipers will worship more with sincere hearts rather than the rituals of past generations.

Some of the evidences of the New Testament worshiper will be actions that are manifestations of changes that are happening inside of their hearts. As Jesus stated, the geographical place of worship can be anywhere. We no longer have to go to the temple, the temple is in us.

Our Temples

We see in 1 Corinthians 3:16-17, *"Know ye not that ye are the temple of God, and that the Spirit of God dwelleth in you? If any man defile the temple of God, him shall God destroy; for the temple of God is holy, which temple ye are."*

Wherever we are or wherever we go, we must remember that His dwelling place is in us. Therefore, we must perform the same maintenance on our bodies that we would have maintained in a temple made with hands.

We must keep our temples cleansed of anything that would defile or make it unpleasing to God.

- Our thoughts must be good thoughts.

Finally, brethren, whatsoever things are true, whatsoever things are honest, whatsoever things are just, whatsoever things are pure, whatsoever things are lovely, whatsoever things are of good report; if there be any virtue, and if there be any praise, think on these things. Those things, which ye have both learned, and received, and heard, and seen in me, do: and the God of peace shall be with you (Philippians 4:8-9).

- Our speech must be clean.

  And he called the multitude, and said unto them, Hear, and understand: not that which goeth into the mouth defileth a man; but that which cometh out of the mouth, this defileth a man (Matthew 15:10-11).

- Our hearts must be clean.
  "Blessed are the pure in heart: for they shall see God (Matthew 5:8)."

  "For God hath not called us unto uncleanness, but unto holiness. He therefore that despiseth, despiseth not man, but God, who hath also given unto us his Holy Spirit (1 Thessalonians 4:7-8)."

Acts of Worship

There are physical acts of worship that distinguish believers who are worshiping in spirit and truth.

- Lifting of hands.
  "I will therefore that men pray every where, lifting up holy hands, without wrath and doubting (1 Timothy 2:8)."

- Giving thanks.

  Be careful for nothing; but in every thing by prayer and supplication with thanksgiving let your requests be made known unto God. And the peace of God, which passeth all understanding, shall keep your hearts and minds through Christ Jesus (Philippians 4:6-7).

  "Giving thanks always for all things unto God and the Father in the name of our Lord Jesus Christ; submitting yourselves one to another in the fear of God (Ephesians 5:20-21)."

- Singing in the Spirit.

  And be not drunk with wine, wherein is excess; but be filled with the Spirit; speaking to yourselves in psalms and hymns and spiritual songs, singing and making melody in your heart to the Lord (Ephesians 5:18-19).

  Let the word of Christ dwell in you richly in all wisdom; teaching and admonishing one another in psalms and hymns and spiritual songs, singing with grace in your hearts to the Lord. And whatsoever ye do in word or deed, do all in the name of the Lord Jesus, giving

*thanks to God and the Father by him
(Colossians 3:16-17).*

• Doing Good.

*By him therefore let us offer the sacri-
fice of praise to God continually, that is,
the fruit of our lips giving thanks to his
name. But to do good and to communi-
cate forget not: for with such sacrifices
God is well pleased (Hebrews 13:15-16).*

History Will Remember Mary

Jesus knew the time of His death was draw-
ing near. The act of worship that Mary had ministered to Jesus was precious to Him. I have heard
many senior citizens say, "Give me flowers while
I am alive so I can appreciate them." Before His
death, Jesus was receiving this special anointing
while He could enjoy the beautiful fragrance and
soothing pleasure of this expensive oil. Jesus
commended Mary and protected her from the verbal attacks of the disciples. She was anointing
Him before His death. Jesus knew that she would
not have opportunity to anoint Him after His
death or at any other time. As far as Jesus was
concerned, her timing was perfect. This anointing was an act of love and honor; Jesus was not
going to let the disciples or Martha spoil it for
Mary.

We read in Mark 14:6-9:

> And Jesus said, Let her alone; why trouble ye her? she hath wrought a good work on me. For ye have the poor with you always, and whensoever ye will ye may do them good: but me ye have not always. She hath done what she could: she is come aforehand to anoint my body to the burying. Verily I say unto you, Wheresoever this gospel shall be preached throughout the whole world, this also that she hath done shall be spoken of for a memorial of her.

Mary not only blessed Jesus, but she established her place in history because of her love and ministry to the Lord. She had developed a love for the Savior that would cause her to be with Him throughout His trials, His beatings, His journey to the cross, His hanging, His death and His burial. She was also one of the first to witness and proclaim His resurrection.

Today popular songs are written about her. Sermons are written and preached about her transformation and loyalty to the Savior. Books are also written about her alabaster box filled with precious oil which she gladly broke and poured over the feet of Jesus. How intimate and loving it was for her to dry the Lord's feet with her hair!

No, Jesus would not let this moment be stolen or taken away from a woman who worshiped Him with all of her heart and soul. Many people have questioned her past and tried to soil her reputation, but Jesus endorsed her act of worship and procured a place of honor and esteem for her in the history of Christianity to which all believers may aspire.

Martha will always be remembered as one who loved and served the Master. She will be remembered as a person who was there to do the work that needed to be done. Work is necessary. James tells us that faith without works is dead. James writes in his epistle, *"Even so faith, if it hath not works, is dead, being alone (James 2:17)."* We accept that truth and work diligently knowing that it is our work that validates our faith.

However, Jesus shows us that works and faith alone will not win the favor of God. The Pharisees had faith and did the works that the Scriptures required of them. They kept the law and performed the traditions and rituals passed down to them from the Mosaic Covenant, but their hearts were far from God. Jesus shows us in Matthew 7:21-23 that works without worship will be meaningless on the Day of Judgment.

> *Not every one that saith unto me, Lord, Lord, shall enter into the kingdom of heaven; but he that doeth the will of my*

Father which is in heaven. Many will say to me in that day, Lord, Lord, have we not prophesied in thy name? and in thy name have cast out devils? and in thy name done many wonderful works? And then will I profess unto them, I never knew you: depart from me, ye that work iniquity.

CHAPTER 11

WORSHIP IN SPIRIT AND TRUTH

Our work assignment must be the result of an intimate worship encounter with God. After salvation, the Holy Spirit comes to live in us and to be intimate with us. As a result of His living in us, we have constant fellowship with Him. The Spirit leads us and guides us in the way of truth and understanding. In John 16:13-15, we read:

> *Howbeit when he, the Spirit of truth, is come, he will guide you into all truth: for he shall not speak of himself; but whatsoever he shall hear, that shall he speak: and he will shew you things to come. He shall glorify me: for he shall*

*receive of mine, and shall shew it unto
you. All things that the Father hath are
mine: therefore said I, that he shall take
of mine, and shall shew it unto you.*

Spirit

Praise invites the presence of God, but worship is the avenue to God's heart. Anyone can praise the Lord. Anyone can say, "Surely there must be a God. Only God could do something like this." However, not just anyone can worship Him. In order to worship Him, you must experience His Holy presence. True worship requires intimacy with God. Worship in spirit and truth is the purest form of worship. Don't get me wrong! I pray every day. The first thing I do in the morning is get up and brush my teeth and seek His face and will for my life throughout the course of that day.

A lot of us pray, but we often pray without worshiping. Prayer is important. But, when we worship God, He always wants to hear how much we love Him. We can't go wrong with worship. We can't go wrong with being intimate and close to Him. We can't go wrong when we worship in spirit. What is spirit? That is the part of our being that communes directly with God. Since we are made in the image of God, humans are triune beings: body, soul and spirit.

The body is flesh and came from the earth. It will decay and return to dust.

The soul consists of an individual's mind, will and emotions. Our intellect, desires and feelings are the products of our soul.

The spirit is that part of us which never dies. In our natural birth we are born under the curse of death, which is separation from God. We are in jeopardy of eternal torment and Jesus came to give us new life.

John writes in his gospel:

Jesus answered and said unto him, Verily, verily, I say unto thee, Except a man be born again, he cannot see the kingdom of God. Nicodemus saith unto him, How can a man be born when he is old? can he enter the second time into his mother's womb, and be born? Jesus answered, Verily, verily, I say unto thee, Except a man be born of water and of the Spirit, he cannot enter into the kingdom of God. That which is born of the flesh is flesh; and that which is born of the Spirit is spirit. Marvel not that I said unto thee, Ye must be born again. The wind bloweth where it listeth, and thou hearest the sound thereof, but canst not tell whence it cometh, and whither it goeth: so is every one that is born of the Spirit (John 3:3-8).

New life in the spirit of Christ is what allows us to have fellowship with God and thus gives us access to eternal life. This is what Christians refer to as the born-again experience. New birth or the born-again experience only comes as a result of receiving Jesus as our personal Savior and living our lives according to His teachings and commandments. The Bible records:

For God so loved the world, that he gave his only begotten Son, that whosoever believeth in him should not perish, but have everlasting life. For God sent not his Son into the world to condemn the world; but that the world through him might be saved. He that believeth on him is not condemned: but he that believeth not is condemned already, because he hath not believed in the name of the only begotten Son of God. And this is the condemnation, that light is come into the world, and men loved darkness rather than light, because their deeds were evil. For every one that doeth evil hateth the light, neither cometh to the light, lest his deeds should be reproved. But he that doeth truth cometh to the light, that his deeds may be made manifest, that they are wrought in God (John 3:16-21).

God desires us to worship Him. *Worship* can be defined as a tribute to a divine being; reverence to one greater than yourself; to kneel or to bow; to kiss in humility; to be intimate and to be close.

What is spirit? God is spirit. It says in John 4:24, *"God is a spirit and those that worship Him must worship Him in spirit and in truth."* The third character of man is the spirit which is the only part that communes with God.

Many times as you read the Word, you see the words *heart* and *spirit* are interchangeable. The Bible refers to the spirit as the heart of man. An example may be seen in Matthew 15:7-9, *"Hypocrites. What did Isaiah prophecy about you saying, these people draw near me with their mouths and honor me with their lips, but their hearts (or spirits) are far from me. In vain they worship me."* Why? This tribute was coming from their mouth and mind, not their heart or spirit. Jesus said, *"In vain they worship me teaching as doctrines the commandments of men."*

Truth

What is truth? Jesus said, *"I am the way, the truth and the life. No one comes to the Father but by me (John 14:6)."* Truth is uncontaminated, unpolluted and unexaggerated. Jesus was saying this, "If you're going to worship the Father, you've got to go through the Son." Imagine you have a father and son living in a house. Suppose a stranger comes to your house and he wants to speak to the father. The father says, "This is my beloved son in whom I'm well-pleased. Everything that I own belongs to him. I'm so pleased with him that when he speaks, it's like me speaking." In fact, this son will not say anything that his father has not already said because he represents his father. This son is the voice of his father. The father has given him all the authority. A stranger comes to the door and wants to see the father. The stranger tells the son, "Move on out of the way, I want to talk to your father, boy." Pushing the son aside, the stranger tries to get to the father.

What is the father going to say after the stranger has already insulted his son? What would the father say? He might say, "I can't see you." Jesus said, "You can't see the Father. You cannot have an audience with Him unless you go by Me because I am the way. I am the truth. If you're going to have a life, you're going to get it through Me." When the son is standing there and the stranger says, "I recognize you as the heir of everything your father has. I recognize you as the authority. I ask your permission. In your name, I would like to go and address the father." You must recognize God's Son. You cannot ignore God's family if you are going to worship Him.

In the Old Testament, worship was all about the slaughter of cattle, sheep, goats, and

birds. Then God decided that the time had come
to make a new covenant. Worship would be done
in a different way. God sent His Son Jesus into
the earth in the form of man. Jesus allowed Himself to be the sacrificial lamb and shed His blood
so that we might be able to approach the Father
individually and bypass the rituals of the high
priests. It's by the blood of God's Son and His suffering that we are able to come to God. We are
able to approach the Father individually or col-
lectively and make our request in the name of
Jesus our Lord. **Praise invites the presence of
God, but worship is the avenue to God's heart.**

CHAPTER 12

PRAISE AND WORSHIP
MY PRIORITY

Humble Beginnings

In the summer of 1944, my mother Edith was in the second pregnancy trimester with her third child. Her husband, Joshua Kenoly, was away in the Pacific Ocean on a U.S. military ship that was engaged in the war with Japan.

She had two older boys: Jerry, 4 and Wendell, 2. They were both high-energy, strong-willed boys who constantly kept her busy and tired.

Her grandmother, Classie Williams, had raised her because her mother had died when she was born. She grew up as an only child, poor and motherless. Her father, Ellis Glover, had been a merchant seaman from his early teens. He was always away at sea and my mother saw him only a few times while she was growing up.

Edith had a relatively lonely childhood with no siblings, no mother, and an absentee father. She only had Grandma Classie who was half black and half Native American. They were poor, uneducated and lonely.

She had always wanted a large family to offset the loneliness she had experienced as a child and she did not want to be a single parent. The nation, on the other hand, was at war and all of the able-bodied young men, including my father, had been drafted to fight in either Europe or the Pacific theaters.

In 1943, my mother, Grandma Classie, Jerry and Wendell had just migrated from Wagoner, Oklahoma to Coffeyville, Kansas at the encouragement of her in-laws.

She had always loved to sing and was very good at it. She joined the Twelfth Street Baptist Church in Coffeyville and soon began singing in the choir. Singing brought joy to her heart and helped her to overcome the fear associated with her young husband being away at sea fighting in the war and the responsibility of her aged grandmother and her two young, active boys.

She only had an eighth grade education and was limited to domestic housework jobs to make ends meet. Music was her only escape from the challenges of life and circumstances. When she sang in church, the sorrow of her experiences and the hope of her faith in God, seemed to come out all at the same time. People could always tell that she had spent time with God. Edith praised and worshiped her way through the hard and difficult times that the 1940's offered to a lonely, young black mother.

In the middle of this third pregnancy, Edith began praying a prayer that would set the course for the life of her unborn child. She would rub her stomach and pray to God, **"Lord, let this one praise you."** I believe that somehow God gives special attention to the prayers of lonely broken-hearted mothers.

I know that God answered my mother's prayers when I was born. James 5:16 says, *"The effectual fervent prayers of the righteous availeth much."* From the time I can remember, I always tried to sing. My mother told me that before I could talk, I would hum myself to sleep. Music has always been in my heart and in my mouth. God answers prayers.

I'm Going To Be A Singer

When I was eight years old, I made a deci-sion that would guide the course of my life forever. We lived on the west side of the Missouri Pacific railroad tracks in Coffeyville. Everyone in our section of town was poor. Our family was among the poorest of the poor. Grandma Classie was nearing the end of her life and I now had a little brother named Joshua (we called him Muffin).

The father of one of my childhood friends was an automobile mechanic. He had his own repair shop and he did better financially than all of the other black men in our little section of town. Televisions had just become affordable for some people and my friend's family was the first black family on our side of town to own one.

Televisions, at that time, had very small screens and were housed in very large wooden cabinets. Color television had not yet been invented so all of the images were black and white. They needed a very tall antenna that seemed to reach half way to heaven. There was only one channel that could be viewed in our town and it was broadcast from Tulsa, Oklahoma which was located some seventy miles directly south of our town. The images were small and fuzzy much of the time depending on the weather.

On summer nights, this family would turn the television towards the window on the side of their house and all of the families in the neighborhood would come over and watch it. Ninety percent of the people on the television were white people. Every now and then, there would be a black person on the screen and we would all celebrate the fact that a black person was on the television.

It seemed that all of the black people on television were cast in some type of demeaning role or negative stereotype. They played the roles of maids, porters, janitors and slaves. Every person of color was always cast at the lowest realm of the social ladder. Since all of the black people that I knew in real life and all of the black people we saw on television were set in these types of menial and humiliating settings, I was beginning to think that type of life was all I had to look forward to in my future.

Hope came to me when I finally saw two black men on the silver screen who were not cast in the usual stereotypical roles. Sammy Davis, Jr. and Nat King Cole were the men that gave hope for a future that seemed so far away, but I wanted it.

These men were respected and celebrated for their gifts and talents. They were respected and held in high esteem for their ability to sing and play music. These men were well-dressed, well-spoken, groomed and seemingly loved by all races. They loved music and music had taken them to levels in life to which other careers could not compare.

That's when I decided that I was going to have a career in music. I was going to be a singer. All other careers were no longer a consideration. I didn't want to be a doctor, lawyer, farmer, policeman, fireman, pilot or anything else. I wanted to be a singer. Music was my dream and my passion. That summer night in the side yard of my friend's house, I made up my mind to become a singer and that quest was birthed in my heart.

Growing Up, God's Hand Was On Me

I grew up singing in the schools and churches that I attended. Thank God for music and physical education classes while I was in high school. Those were the only classes in which I received "A"s. Music helped me stay in school.

My two older brothers had dropped out of high school and joined the U. S. Marine Corps. For a while I thought that I would follow that same path, but my mother encouraged me to stay in school. Even though my grades were poor, I had a chance to be the first person in my immediate family to graduate from high school.

My music classes were my favorite classes in high school. I was involved in every musical event that my teacher would allow me to participate. I was not even close to being one of the best singers in the choir, but no one loved to sing more than me. I sang in the baritone-bass section of the school choir and enjoyed every minute of every class.

In my junior and senior years at Coffeyville High School, I entered vocal contests that were sponsored by the school district and the state of Kansas. In my junior year, I won first place in my category of the district finals. In my senior year, I won first place in the state competition.

The Union Baptist Church was the place where I really learned the most. I grew up in that church and sang in the choir. The church was small with less than one hundred members. Our choir consisted of about twenty adults and teens.

My mother was one of the soloists in that choir and was very good. Everyone loved her soprano voice and her ability to stir up the church emotionally. Shouting and dancing were normal exercises in our services and she was the catalyst for most of it. She loved music and she loved God. When she sang I knew that it was coming from deep within her soul because I knew of the pain and heartache that she was going through. I knew that she was a praying mother because I saw her pray and I witnessed God's answer to many of her prayers.

My finishing high school was an answer to one of my mother's prayers. I graduated in May, 1962 and we moved to Tulsa, Oklahoma two days after my graduation. I owe thanks to several people who made great deposits in my life. There were men who taught me things that my absentee father should have taught me. My pastor, Russell Nuckols, taught me how to develop a work ethic. C.D. Fisher, my church choir director, taught me how to select music and be sensitive to the Holy Spirit. Mr. Bass, my high school choir director, helped me to overcome the fear of competition.

At the time they were teaching me, I didn't know the importance of the life lessons they were imparting to me. I know now that God had His hand on me and was covering me all through the early years of my life. I can see how God protected me and surrounded me with people who would help shape my character and moral fiber.

Journey To The Stars

I joined the U. S. Air Force in 1964 and served for three years. I was stationed in Northern California at Travis Air Force Base. During the time I served in the military, I also sang with local rock and soul bands in area night clubs. It was in the Air Force that I met and married Tavita. Our first son, Tony, was born in 1968 and not long after his birth we moved to Los Angeles, California.

Through a radio talent contest, I won a record contract that started me on my way to fulfilling my childhood dreams. I recorded for several major record labels for the next seven years. I had several recordings that were local hits, but I never had that big blockbuster hit that could take a career over the top. However, I was getting closer to my dream.

I was attaining all the goals that I set for myself. However, after reaching my goals, they didn't bring the satisfaction that I hoped they would bring. I was singing every night. I was making good money. I hung out with well-known celebrity friends and was well-respected by all of my peers in the music industry. On the surface it seemed like I was on top of the world, but deep inside my heart I was miserable. My quest for stardom had caused me to neglect my beautiful and faithful wife and son. I was not the same young man that grew up in Coffeyville in a Christian home and environment. I was fast becoming one of the self-centered, greedy, egotistical people that Hollywood is famous for producing.

Tavita and I had separated several times and our marriage was headed for divorce. One Sunday morning in the spring of 1975, she rededicated her life to the Lord and began praying for our marriage to be healed. She became a faithful church member and got involved with prayer circles at Angeles Temple Church in Los Angeles.

I could see that my life was headed for disaster if I continued on the path for stardom. I was surrounded with all of the sinful things that I had been taught to avoid when I was growing up. Drugs, perversion, stealing, promiscuity, backbiting and many other ungodly things were going on around me. I soon realized that If I didn't get out of the rat race that I was in, I was going to destroy myself or something was going to destroy me.

I loved music. But I had to make a choice between music and my family. I didn't want to lose my wife and son. I didn't want my wife and son to go through what my mother went through when I was growing up in Coffeyville. On November 19, 1975 I rededicated my life to Jesus and made a decision to live my life for Him.

Making A New Start

It was still going to take a few years to satisfy the terms of the recording contracts that I had signed. However, I was determined to live a life that was pleasing before the Lord and commit whatever gifts and talents I had for service in the Kingdom of God. The Lord intervened and caused my producer to release me from my contract. This allowed me to move to Oakland, California and try to start my life over with Jesus as Lord of my life.

My mother invited my young family to move in with her and two of my brothers. There were five adults and two children living in a two bedroom house. We lived like this for several months. I worked handyman jobs and any kind of work that I could find to bring income into the household.

In the fall of 1976, I was hired as a locker room attendant at a local community college. It was often embarrassing and humiliating when students would recognize me and tease me about being a person who had hit records, but was working a minimum wage job in a locker room. The former pride I possessed was crushed and trampled by the remarks of the students at the college.

Several secular record companies had heard I was not under a present contract. They got in touch with me and made offers for me to return to Los Angeles and record for them. I must admit that I was tempted to accept their offers. However, when the Holy Spirit would remind me of the promise I had made to the Lord, I refused them all. I finally settled it in my heart that I was never going back to the life that I was living in Los Angeles. Jesus said in Luke 9:62, *"Any man who sets his hands to the plow and looks back is not fit for the Kingdom."* I was finished with the old life and moved toward the hope and promises that are in Christ Jesus.

From The Locker Room To The Classroom

I enrolled in night school and earned a degree in music in the spring of 1978. The Dean of my department at the College of Alameda arranged for me to apply for an eminence degree in music and teach some courses in the music department or our school. My professional experience and accomplishments in the music industry along with my newly earned degree in music qualified me to teach some courses at the community colleges. After completing some vocational teaching courses at the University of California at Berkeley, I received a lifetime credential to teach music in the state of California from kindergarten through high school, including some college classes. I immediately was hired to teach in the music department of the same school in which I had been working for the past two years.

God was beginning to elevate me because of my faithfulness to the commitment that I had made to Him. Between the months of May and September in 1978, I was promoted from the locker room to the classroom. Many of the students who teased me in the locker room were now some of my students. Right away my classes became the most popular classes in the music department.

My students were hungry to learn from someone who had done what they were trying to do. They wanted to go where I had been in the world of popular music. I was not only able to teach them, but also impart to them life lessons and wisdom they would need to experience success in a music career.

I was not only able to teach them, but I was able to witness to them and share the love of God. In my classrooms, I was able to help hundreds of young people apply the wisdom of God to the life-changing decisions that were before them. They trusted me and allowed me to speak into their lives. The testimony of my promotion from the locker room to the classroom, which many of them had witnessed, was enough to lead many of them to Christ.

I was beginning to see that God had more in His plan for my life than just being a singer. Music was the key that would open the doors to many opportunities of ministry that God had in store for my life. I enjoyed being able to help people with life issues. I loved sharing my testimony and leading people to Jesus. The more I learned, the more I realized that there was so much more to learn. I loved it all. It seemed like I had passed through the dark night of the soul.

Miracle Children

After our first son was born, Tavita had two miscarriages. The doctors told her that she had damaged her female organs and would never have any more children. Of course, we didn't receive that report; we believed the report of the Lord. We wanted more children and God promised that He would give us the desires of our hearts if we would trust in Him. So we trusted Him and God healed Tavita and gave us two more beautiful, strong-willed, high-energy, healthy boys: Ronald Joshua and Samuel Ramon. Their births were miracle births.

Tavita and I both came from large families and we both wanted several children. All three of our boys were caesarian deliveries so we agreed that we didn't want her to be cut anymore and we stopped at three. At the time of this writing, they are all grown and serving the Lord. Hallelujah!

The Purging of My Soul

Tavita and I bought a little house and made it our sanctuary. The windows were boarded up and it needed work done on it when we moved in, but we loved it. It was a house of love and prayer.

I began to get really serious about song-writing. As I studied the Word of God, He would give me songs directly from the Scriptures. The songs that I received from the Lord were songs of victory, overcoming, and authority in the Word of God. The songs were full of joy and gladness. They were songs of hope and inspiration. Many of the songs produce an awesome awareness of the presence of God.

In the late 1970's, no one called church music *praise and worship*. To me, it was just music that I felt in my heart that God wanted to hear. I didn't know of any churches that were doing the kind of music in their services that I was writing. At the time, I thought I was the only one writing music that way.

The leaders of the church that I attended told me the music that I was writing and wanted to sing in the services was disliked and unwanted. I sent demos to all of the Christian record companies and all of them rejected me. For several years I attempted to get people in the Christian music industry to accept my music, but it seemed like I was either before my time or my time had passed.

Captive Audience

In 1977, one of my brothers was in some trouble with the law. He was sentenced to serve five years in the Washington State Correctional Facility. I started taking days off to visit him and encourage him. While serving his time, he repented and made peace with God. He began attending chapel services and was really focusing on the things of God and reconstructing his life.

He told the chaplain of the institution that I could sing and had written several songs. The chaplain invited me to come and sing my songs

117

to the inmates of his congregation. I was delighted. Finally, someone wanted to hear the songs the Lord had given to me.

I organized a group of local musicians and singers and named them the *Cedars of Lebanon*. We practiced and prepared ourselves to go on this fifteen hour trip from Northern California to Eastern Washington to sing and play for Jesus. This trip would prove to be a major event for all of us because none of us had ever been in a maximum security institution. Most of the members experienced some fears and anxieties; they were all relatively new to public performances and Christian ministry. I had the most experience as a singer, but had sung Christian music only a few times outside of a Christian environment.

We were a brand new group with new songs and going into an environment that was completely foreign and intimidating. When we went through the inspection area and passed through the gate that separated us from the outside free world, all of us knew that we were crossing a threshold from a good idea to a God idea. Encouraging those that are in prison is one of the passions of Christ. He talked about visiting those who are in prison in Matthew 25:34-40:

> *Then shall the King say unto them on*
> *his right hand, Come, ye blessed of my*
> *Father, inherit the kingdom prepared*

*for you from the foundation of the
world: for I was an hungred, and ye gave
me meat: I was thirsty, and ye gave me
drink: I was a stranger, and ye took me
in: naked, and ye clothed me: I was sick,
and ye visited me: I was in prison, and
ye came unto me. Then shall the righteous answer him, saying, Lord, when
saw we thee an hungred, and fed thee?
or thirsty, and gave thee drink? When
saw we thee a stranger, and took thee
in? or naked, and clothed thee? Or
when saw we thee sick, or in prison, and
came unto thee? And the King shall answer and say unto them, Verily I say
unto you, Inasmuch as ye have done it
unto one of the least of these my
brethren, ye have done it unto me.*

We were about to become real ministers.
We were not ordained or licensed, but we were
doing the will of God. With our equipment set up,
we began to sing and play our music. There were
about fifty inmates sitting together all in their
blue denim prison uniforms. They all seemed to
have hard cold looks on their faces, except my
brother. Our visit there was going to make him
very popular among his fellow inmates and, of
course, he was glad to see me.

I began to lead the songs that we had prepared for the inmates, but they could hear the

anxiety in my voice and and see the anxiety in my countenance. I began to pray as I was singing and ask the Holy Spirit to help me. The fear soon disappeared and I could see a breakthrough as the inmate congregation began to clap their hands and sing along with the simple choruses of the songs. It was then that I realized that God was starting me out in ministry with a captive audience.

When we had used up our allocated time, I invited the prisoners to receive Jesus as their personal Savior and several of them raised their hands and prayed the prayer of faith with me. My breakthrough had finally come. God was using me and my new group of singers and musicians.

That chaplain told other chaplains about me and our group, and those chaplains told other people and parachurch organizations about us. For the next four years, we were ministering up and down the west coast of America in prisons, parks, schools, military bases and small churches. A new season of my life had begun.

A New Season

As time went by, our group gained a small amount of recognition in the Northern California area for being a group with serious, sincere ministry potential. I felt as though the Christian record companies would now be interested in my music. Again, I tried with no success to acquire a deal that would take my music to the radio stations and record shops. However, there was no difference in the responses from the Christian labels that I solicited. They still didn't want me or my music.

I was at a real low emotional point. Suffering from disappointment and rejection, I felt like there was no place in the body of Christ for those songs that God had given to me. At the same time, there were still secular record companies offering me the old life of singing secular music, but my heart was set and my mind was fixed on the things of God. I was not going to return to a life which I knew would bring eventual disaster for my soul.

God knew that I was hurting. He could see that all I wanted to do was to serve Him with my whole heart. The Lord knew I was willing to follow Him wherever He would lead me.

The year was 1982 and it was a hot summer night in the month of August. Tavita and I were now attending the little Foursquare church directly across the street from our house. East Oakland had one of the worst crime and violence records in the nation. There were many break-ins in our neighborhood and several of them were at our church. My pastor had given me a key to the church so that I could respond to the police whenever the church alarm went off.

One a Saturday evening, I went to have a talk with God in our empty church. I wasn't angry with the Lord, but I did want to reason with Him and get some understanding about what was going on in my life. God invites us to come and reason with Him. Isaiah 1:18 says, *"Come now, and let us reason together, saith the Lord: though your sins be as scarlet, they shall be as white as snow; though they be red like crimson, they shall be as wool."*

I had serious questions about where my life was going. If I was wasting my time trying to make something happen in Christian music, I wanted to change. Was this the life that God had ordained for me? Was I wasting my time? Should I abandon my childhood dreams and try another career to support my family?

I was not trying to get the Lord to do what I wanted in my life; I wanted to do what He wanted me to do. I just needed to know if music was what He had planned for my life. Was music my calling? Was music my ministry? It was time to have a little talk with Jesus.

When I unlocked the door and entered the sanctuary, I began to pray. I locked the door behind me and was not going to open it for anyone. This was a special time for me to be alone with God.

I remember saying to the Father, "Lord, all of my life I have tried to sing. From the time I was a little child I've had music in my heart and my mouth. You put music in my heart. You put this desire in me to make music and write songs. These songs that I have written are about You. They are straight from Your Holy Word. These songs praise and exalt You; they are songs of love and adoration to You. Each one tells about Your goodness and greatness. They are simple, but well-written like the Psalms. With these songs, people can sing these songs together and glorify You in Your church."

I continued my prayer, "It seems that hardly anyone wants these songs. Almost everyone rejects me and the music. You gave this music to me and I'm giving it back to you."

I sat down at the piano and began to sing these simple songs back to the Lord. I sang every song that I could play and several that I couldn't play. I sang them anyway. The songs seem to come from deep within my soul. I was experiencing levels of emotions that I had never experienced before. Suddenly the sanctuary was filled with an awesome presence of the Lord. I closed my eyes and continued to sing and worship Him. My eyes remained closed because I was overwhelmed with His presence and I felt unworthy to ever try to look at Him. He was there. I knew

He was there. I didn't have to see Him with my eyes; I knew it with my heart.

At one point, I felt a peace and an unusual comfort as I lay face down on the floor. I don't even remember when I left the piano bench and lay prostrate with my face in the carpet. I could feel Him smiling at me. I could sense His pleasure and favor.

I lay on the floor for what seemed to be a long time; I lost all track of time. I had stopped crying and a sense of joy flooded my heart like never before. My face was in a pool of tears on the wet carpet, but it didn't matter. I was in a spiritual place where I had never been before. I experienced a realm of spirituality that I didn't know existed.

When I finally did get up from the floor I realized that I had advanced to a new level in my walk with God. I knew that through worship I had touched the heart of God. I knew that He was pleased with me. He really did like my songs. He received my offerings of worship and praise. I had a personal and direct affirmation from God Himself that I was born to praise and worship Him. He had made me the person that my mother prayed I would be.

When I walked out of that church I was a changed man. It didn't matter if churches didn't want to hear or sing my songs; God liked them. It didn't matter if the record and publishing companies rejected me anymore; God affirmed me. The approval of others no longer mattered because God Himself had smiled on me and let me know that His favor was upon me.

Worship had brought me into the presence of God. It wouldn't matter if I never sang in a church again because I had sung to the One who created music and He received my songs. Record companies didn't matter because I knew that my songs were now recorded in the heart of God. On that hot August night, it no longer mattered if the earthly audiences disapproved of me because I had just ministered to the greatest audience of all eternity, the King of Glory.

Where Do You Go From Here?

What next? After leaving that church I knew what I had experienced was something that God wanted all of His children to experience. God wants us all to know Him in that same personal and intimate way. He is not a respecter of persons. The love, acceptance and forgiveness that I had found through worship was something that every believer needs to experience. God desires that same kind of encounter with Him for all of us. He wants to be with us. He wants us to touch His heart with our love and adoration. The Lord wants us to pursue His heart with passion and determination to touch Him. He invites us to come. When we draw near to Him, He draws near to us.

My priority is to help others come to Him and know what it's like to have His smile and favor. King David enlists us to magnify the Lord and exalt His name together. Psalms 34:6 says, *"O magnify the Lord with me, and let us exalt his name together."*

Since that Saturday night in August 1982, worship has been the priority of my life. I live a life of worship and encourage others to magnify the Lord with me. Music is one of the vehicles that is used to help us to worship in spirit and truth. As I stated earlier in this book, **worship is more than just the music that we sing and play, it is about touching the heart of God with our expressions of love and adoration. It is about an encounter with God that transcends time, space, language, culture, social strata, economics, race, heritage, denominations and age.**

Go Into All The World

After that night, God opened opportunities for me that caused my ministry to advance in a way that only He could. Well-known speakers would come to Northern California and ask for me by name to lead praise and worship at their meetings. I started traveling around the country on a regular basis with evangelist Mario Murillo.

Soon afterwards I was hired by Pastor Dick Bernal to be the music director at Jubilee Christian Center in San Jose, California. My service there attracted the attention of Don Moen of Integrity Music and soon afterwards I became a worship leader for the Hosanna series of praise and worship recordings.

Since that time, the music I record has literally gone all over the world. At the time of this writing, our ministry has visited ninety-two nations and there is no major populated geographical area on planet earth that we have not been invited to for praise and worship services or teaching about praise and worship.

I have come to realize that I was created to worship the Lord and lead others to do the same. I was created to praise Him. Praising God was the prayer of my mother and has become the passion of my life. Everyone has a purpose in life and many have yet to find their true purpose. I thank God that I have found mine. My passion and my priority are one and the same: praise and worship of our most high and wonderful God.

RON KENOLY MINISTRIES

Dr. Ron Kenoly and the RKM Worship Team are interested in ministering in your city. If you are interested in hosting an event with our team, please allow the following steps to guide you through the process.

  • Fax or mail RKM an official letter of invitation on your ministry letterhead.
Fax: 407.226.2917
Mail: P. O. Box 2200, Windermere, FL 34786 USA

  • The RKM Events Department will respond to your invitation by faxing you an Events Detail Questionnaire and Hosts Responsibility Form. This will give you more information regarding the travel, lodging and financial goals of our Ministry Team.

  • After these communications, your contact person and our Events Department will be able to work out details for a successful Ministry Event.

Email Events Coordinator at *events@RonKenoly.org.*

Ron Kenoly's

Academy of Praise

Training Mentoring Imparting

Dr. Ron Kenoly invites you to join him for intense sessions of training, mentoring and imparting at his Academy of Praise. Each session is designed to take you to a higher level of excellence and effectiveness in your worship leading experience and ministry. Every class will be a journey into God's presence. Receive proven answers to the most common and uncommon issues from one of the nation's leading praise and worship authorities.

The day sessions will end with personal prayer, laying on of hands and the presentation of a certificate of completion. Don't miss your opportunity to be part of this exciting week.

REGISTER TODAY!

Visit www.RonKenoly.org for more details.

Parsons Publishing House
Your Voice Your World™

Parsons Publishing House
P. O. Box 6428
Panama City FL 32404
Tel: 850.867.3061

Info@ParsonsPublishingHouse.com
www.ParsonsPublishingHouse.com

ORDER ADDITIONAL COPIES

The PRIORITY OF PRAISE & WORSHIP
by Dr. Ron Kenoly

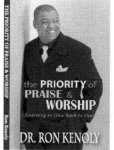

Ron Kenoly has stepped into a new season of ministry where his heart and vision is to mentor worship leaders, pastors and worshipers. Through this book, you will receive proven answers to common and uncommon issues from one of the nation's most anointed and experienced worship leading authorities. Each chapter is designed to take you to a higher level of excellence and effectiveness in your worship experience. Order your additional copies today for only $12.95 + $3 S/H.

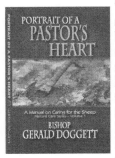